MOTHER'S BOY

The True Story of Ed Gein and the Making of a Monster

By R.M. Cochran

First Edition

Copyright Page

MOTHER'S BOY: The True Story of Ed Gein and the Making of a Monster

Copyright © 2025 by R.M. Cochran

All rights reserved. No part of this publication may be reproduced, distributed, or transmitted in any form or by any means, including photocopying, recording, or other electronic or mechanical methods, without the prior written permission of the publisher, except in the case of brief quotations embodied in critical reviews and certain other noncommercial uses permitted by copyright law.
First Edition: 2025

Publisher: 1776 Publishing
Printed in the United States of America

Table of Contents

Dedication

Introduction

Chapter 1: The Last Customer

Chapter 2: The House of Horrors

Chapter 3: Mother's Boy

Chapter 4: Brothers in Shadow

Chapter 5: The Death of Everything

Chapter 6: The Final Hunt

Chapter 7: Inside the Nightmare

Chapter 8: The Trial of a Monster

Chapter 9: The Making of a Legend

Chapter 10: The End of a Monster

Dedication

To the memory of Mary Hogan and Bernice Worden, whose lives were tragically cut short

*And to their
families, who
have carried
the burden of
these losses
with dignity
and grace*

Introduction

On a cold November evening in 1957, Sheriff Art Schley pushed open the door of a small outbuilding behind an isolated farmhouse in Plainfield, Wisconsin, and discovered something that would haunt him for the rest of his life. Hanging from the rafters, dressed like a deer, was the decapitated and gutted corpse of Bernice Worden, a respected local businesswoman who had disappeared from her hardware store earlier that day. But the horror of that discovery would pale in comparison to what investigators found when they entered the main farmhouse. There, scattered throughout rooms filled with accumulated debris, was a collection of household items that defied comprehension: bowls made from human skulls, lampshades crafted from faces, furniture upholstered with human skin, and a "woman suit" constructed from the torsos of female victims.

The man responsible for these unthinkable acts was Ed Gein, a fifty-one-year-old bachelor farmer who had lived quietly among his neighbors for decades. To the residents of Plainfield, he had seemed harmless—eccentric perhaps, but polite and helpful when called upon. No one suspected that behind his mild demeanor lay a mind so damaged that it had turned to murder and grave robbing to satisfy psychological needs that normal people could barely imagine.

The Ed Gein case would become one of the most influential criminal investigations in American history, not because of the number of victims—he confessed to killing only two people—but because of the unprecedented nature of his crimes and their lasting impact on popular culture.

Chapter 1:
The Last Customer

November 16, 1957 - 7:43 PM

Sheriff Art Schley had seen plenty of blood in his twenty-three years of law enforcement, but he'd never seen anything like this. The beam of his flashlight cut through the darkness of the small shed behind the Gein farmhouse, illuminating what appeared to be a human body hanging upside down from the rafters like a butchered deer.
But this wasn't a deer.

The body had been decapitated and gutted, suspended by ropes tied around the ankles. Where the head should have been, there was only empty space and dried blood. The torso had been split open from sternum to pelvis, cleaned out with the precision of someone who knew exactly what they were doing.

"Jesus Christ," Deputy Peck whispered behind him, his voice barely audible in the frigid air.

Schley forced himself to look closer, though every instinct screamed at him to turn away. This was Bernice Worden. The woman who had sold him hardware supplies for years, who had asked about his wife just last month, who had become the center of a frantic search when she disappeared from her store earlier that day. What they had found in this ramshackle shed would haunt Schley for the rest of his life. But it was only the beginning.

Twelve Hours Earlier - 7:30 AM

The day had started like any other in Plainfield, Wisconsin. Snow fell steadily on the small farming community, adding to the blanket of white that had transformed the countryside into a picture-perfect winter scene. Main Street was quiet in the early morning hours, with only a few pickup trucks parked outside the diner where farmers gathered for coffee before heading out to their fields.

Bernice Worden unlocked the front door of her hardware store at exactly 8:00 AM, just as she had every weekday for the past fifteen years. At fifty-eight, she was a fixture in the community — a no-nonsense businesswoman who had earned the respect of every farmer in Waushara County.

Her husband had left her the store when he died, and she'd proven more than capable of running it on her own. The brass bell above the door chimed softly as she entered, its familiar sound echoing through the cluttered interior. Shelves lined every wall from floor to ceiling, packed with everything a farming community could need: tools, hardware, feed, hunting supplies, and household goods. The smell of motor oil and fertilizer permeated the air, mixed with the distinctive scent of new leather and rubber. Behind the wooden counter sat a massive brass cash register, its ornate Victorian design a testament to the store's long history.

Bernice went through her morning routine methodically. She checked the heat, turned on the lights, and reviewed the previous day's sales in the ledger she kept beside the register. Business had been steady despite the harsh winter — farmers always needed supplies, regardless of the weather.
She had no way of knowing that this would be the last morning she would ever unlock that door.

By 9:15 AM, the first customers of the day began to arrive. Harold Thompson stopped by for fence wire. Mrs. Anderson needed a new coffee pot. Young Billy Fletcher picked up ammunition for his father's hunting rifle. Each transaction was recorded in Bernice's neat handwriting in the sales ledger, along with the time and amount.

At 9:30 AM, the bell chimed again. This time, the customer who entered was someone Bernice knew well, though not necessarily someone she was comfortable being alone with. Ed Gein shuffled through the door, his thin frame bundled in an old coat that had seen better days. At fifty-one, he was a familiar figure around Plainfield — the quiet bachelor farmer who lived alone in a deteriorating farmhouse two miles outside town.

"Morning, Ed," Bernice said with the professional courtesy she showed all her customers, though there was something about Gein that had always made her uneasy. He had a way of staring that was just a little too intense, and his conversation often took odd turns. "Morning, Mrs. Worden," Gein replied in his soft, almost feminine voice. "Mighty cold out there today." "What can I help you with?"
"Need some antifreeze. Half-gallon should do it."

Bernice nodded and walked to the automotive section, pulling a red container from the shelf. It was a routine transaction — antifreeze was a common purchase during Wisconsin winters. She carried it back to the counter and recorded the sale in her ledger: "9:30 AM - Antifreeze - $1.85."

What happened next would remain a mystery that investigators would piece together from physical evidence and the disturbed ramblings of a killer. But what they knew for certain was this: Ed Gein did not simply pay for his antifreeze and leave. Instead, he committed an act of violence so brutal and calculated that it would shock even hardened law enforcement officers.

The details of Bernice Worden's final moments would emerge slowly, through crime scene evidence and Gein's eventual confession. She had been shot in the back of the head with a .22 caliber rifle—a weapon Gein had taken from the store's own inventory. The killing was not spontaneous; it was planned. Gein had been thinking about this moment for days, possibly weeks.

After shooting her, Gein had loaded her body into his pickup truck along with the brass cash register. He'd made a hasty attempt to clean up the blood, but the evidence of what had occurred was impossible to completely erase. Dark stains marked the wooden floor behind the counter, and a trail of droplets led from the scene of the shooting to the back door where Gein had made his escape.

But for the residents of Plainfield going about their Saturday morning routines, life continued normally. No one noticed that Worden's Hardware had closed earlier than usual. No one saw Ed Gein's battered pickup truck speeding down the country roads toward his isolated farm. No one could have imagined that their quiet, eccentric neighbor had just committed murder.

5:32 PM - The Discovery

The call came into the Waushara County Sheriff's office just as the sun was setting behind a wall of gray clouds. Deputy Frank Worden had gone to check on his mother when she failed to come home for dinner, and what he'd found at the hardware store had sent a chill down his spine that had nothing to do with the winter weather.

"Art, I need you to get down here right away," Frank said when Sheriff Schley answered the phone. Despite his training as a law enforcement officer, there was an edge to his voice that Schley had never heard before. "Something's happened to Mom."

Sheriff Arthur Schley had been Waushara County's top lawman for nearly a decade, and he'd developed a reputation for calm competence in handling the minor crimes that occasionally disrupted the peace of this rural community. Bar fights, domestic disputes, the occasional burglary — these were the types of cases that typically crossed his desk. But the tone in Frank Worden's voice suggested something far more serious.

Schley arrived at the hardware store within minutes, his patrol car's headlights cutting through the gathering darkness. The familiar storefront looked normal from the outside, but Frank was waiting by the front door with an expression that made Schley's stomach tighten. "What do we have?" Schley asked as he approached. "She's gone, Art. The register's missing, and there's blood." Frank's professional composure was holding, but barely. "Lots of blood."

The two men entered the store together, and immediately Schley could see what had alarmed the deputy. Behind the wooden counter, dark stains marked the floor in an irregular pattern. Some appeared to be droplets, others looked like someone had tried to wipe up larger pools of blood and hadn't been entirely successful.

Schley pulled out his flashlight and examined the scene more carefully. The bloodstains told a story — someone had been shot or struck behind the counter, probably near where the cash register normally sat. The missing register suggested robbery as a motive, but the amount of blood indicated that whoever had been injured here had been seriously hurt, possibly killed. "When did you last talk to her?" Schley asked.

"This morning around seven. She said she'd be home by five-thirty for dinner. When she didn't show up, I figured something must have happened." Frank's voice was steady, but his hands were shaking slightly. "The front door was unlocked when I got here, but all the lights were off."

Schley followed the trail of blood droplets with his flashlight beam. They led from behind the counter, through the store, and out the back door. Outside, tire tracks were visible in the snow — someone had backed a vehicle up to the rear entrance and loaded something heavy into it.
"Frank, I need you to think carefully," Schley said. "Who was the last person you know of who saw your mother today?"
"I don't know for sure, but..." Frank paused, considering. "Ed Gein was asking about antifreeze a couple of days ago. Mom mentioned it."

The name hung in the air between them. Everyone in Plainfield knew Ed Gein, though most people tried to avoid prolonged contact with him if they could help it. He was odd — there was no other way to put it. He lived alone on a run-down farm, rarely socialized, and had some peculiar habits that made people uncomfortable. But odd wasn't the same as dangerous. Or so they had always assumed.

"Let's check the sales ledger," Schley suggested.

Frank led him back to the counter, carefully avoiding the bloodstains on the floor. The ledger lay open beside where the cash register had been, and the last entry was clearly visible in Bernice's neat handwriting: "9:30 AM - Antifreeze - $1.85."
There was no customer name recorded, but both men knew that Bernice was meticulous about her record-keeping. If someone had purchased antifreeze that morning, it would have been the last sale of the day. Everything that happened afterward had prevented her from recording any additional transactions.
"We need to pay Ed Gein a visit," Schley said grimly.

7:15 PM - The Gein Farm

The drive to the Gein farmhouse took them down increasingly isolated country roads, past snow-covered fields and stands of bare trees that looked like skeletal fingers against the darkening sky. The farm sat at the end of a rutted dirt lane, approximately two miles from the nearest neighbor.
As their headlights swept across the property, both men could see why Ed Gein was considered the local eccentric. The farmhouse was a two-story structure that might have been impressive once, but decades of neglect had taken their toll. Paint peeled from the wooden siding, several windows were boarded up, and the front porch sagged under the weight of accumulated junk.

Outbuildings dotted the property—a barn, a chicken coop, what appeared to be a summer kitchen, and several smaller sheds. None of them looked to be in much better condition than the main house. Rusted farm equipment sat abandoned in the yard, slowly being reclaimed by weeds and weather.

"Place gives me the creeps," Frank muttered as they pulled up to the house.

Schley couldn't disagree. There was something unsettling about the property that went beyond simple neglect. It felt abandoned, as if the very life had been drained out of it years ago.

They didn't have to look for Ed Gein—he appeared from one of the outbuildings as soon as their car doors slammed shut. In the beam of Schley's flashlight, he looked exactly as always: thin, slightly stooped, wearing clothes that had seen better days. But there was something different about his demeanor. Instead of his usual awkward friendliness, he seemed nervous, almost agitated.

"Evening, Ed," Sheriff Schley called out. "We need to ask you a few questions." "Questions about what?" Gein's voice had its usual soft, almost childlike quality, but there was a wariness there that hadn't been present in their previous encounters.

"Bernice Worden's missing. When's the last time you saw her?"

Gein was quiet for a long moment, and in that silence, both officers sensed they were dealing with something more serious than a simple missing person case.
"I haven't seen Mrs. Worden in quite a while," Gein finally said. "Been visiting my neighbor, Henry Hill, most of the day. You can ask him."

But even as he spoke, Schley noticed that Gein kept glancing toward the small outbuilding he'd emerged from when they arrived. There was something about his body language—the way he positioned himself between the officers and that particular structure—that suggested he was trying to direct their attention away from it.

"Ed, would you mind if we took a look around?" Schley asked. It was phrased as a request, but both men understood it wasn't really optional. Gein hesitated for just a fraction of a second too long. "I suppose that would be all right. But you won't find anything interesting here."

The emphasis he placed on the word "here" struck both officers as odd, as if he was making a very specific denial about this particular location while leaving open the possibility that something might be found elsewhere.

Schley decided to start with the building Gein seemed most anxious about—the small structure that locals knew as a summer kitchen, used for canning and food preparation during the warmer months. Light was seeping through gaps in the wooden walls, suggesting that someone had been working inside recently.

"What's in there, Ed?" Schley asked, nodding toward the summer kitchen.

"Oh, just... you know. Old junk. Nothing important." But as they approached the building, a smell became apparent—something sweet and metallic that made both officers' stomachs turn. It was a smell they both recognized from crime scenes and hunting trips: the unmistakable odor of blood and death. Schley pushed open the wooden door and shined his flashlight inside. What he saw would haunt him for the rest of his life.

Hanging from the rafters by ropes tied around the ankles was the decapitated, gutted corpse of Bernice Worden. She had been dressed like a deer, cleaned and prepared with the same methodical precision that any hunter would use on game. Her head was missing, and the body cavity had been completely cleaned out. "Frank, don't look," Schley said sharply, but it was too late. The deputy had already seen enough to understand what they were dealing with.

Behind them, Ed Gein stood quietly, no longer making any attempt to appear innocent or surprised. When Schley turned to face him, Gein simply nodded, as if acknowledging that his secret had finally been discovered.
"Ed Gein, you're under arrest for the murder of Bernice Worden," Schley said, his voice steady despite the horror of what he'd just witnessed.

As they handcuffed the soft-spoken farmer, neither officer could have imagined that what they'd discovered was only the beginning. The full extent of Ed Gein's crimes—and the unthinkable things they would find inside his farmhouse—would soon shock not just the residents of Plainfield, but the entire nation.

The quiet bachelor farmer who helped his neighbors and tipped his hat to ladies had been hiding a secret so dark, so unthinkable, that it would redefine America's understanding of human evil. And it had all started twelve years earlier, with the death of the one person who had controlled every aspect of his existence: his mother, Augusta Gein.# Chapter 1: The Last Customer

Plainfield, Wisconsin - December 16, 1957

In the heart of Wisconsin's farming country, where everyone knows everyone and doors are rarely locked, Saturday mornings at Worden's Hardware Store followed a predictable rhythm. Farmers would stop by for last-minute supplies, neighbors would catch up on local gossip, and Bernice Worden — a respected businesswoman in her late fifties — would greet each customer with the kind of genuine warmth that small-town proprietors are known for.
But this particular Saturday morning would shatter that peaceful routine forever.

It was just after 9:30 AM when the bell above the front door chimed, announcing what would become the most significant customer interaction in the store's history. The man who entered was familiar to everyone in Plainfield — a quiet, soft-spoken bachelor farmer named Ed Gein. At fifty-one years old, Gein was known around town as something of an oddball, but harmless enough. He lived alone on a rundown farm outside town, rarely socialized, and had a habit of showing up at local establishments at odd hours.

What happened next would take investigators years to fully understand, but the basic facts were simple enough: Ed Gein purchased a half-gallon of antifreeze, paid in cash, and left the store. Bernice Worden was never seen alive again.

By 5:30 that evening, when Bernice failed to return home and her son Frank—a deputy sheriff—discovered blood on the floor of the empty hardware store, a nightmare was about to unfold that would challenge everything the people of Plainfield thought they knew about their quiet neighbor.

Because Ed Gein, the soft-spoken farmer who tipped his hat to ladies and helped neighbors with their chores, had been hiding a secret so dark, so unthinkable, that it would inspire decades of horror movies and forever change how America understood the monsters that could live among us.

The truth about what Ed Gein had been doing in the farmhouse where he lived alone would prove to be far more terrifying than any work of fiction. And it all began to unravel on that snowy December morning when he walked into Worden's Hardware Store for the last time.

5:32 PM - Same Day

The phone call that would change everything came just as Sheriff Art Schley was preparing to head home for the weekend. On the other end of the line was Deputy Frank Worden, and the professional composure in his voice couldn't mask the underlying tension.

"Art, I need you to come down to the hardware store. Something's wrong. Mom's missing, and there's... there's blood." In a town like Plainfield, where violent crime was virtually nonexistent, those words carried an almost surreal quality. Blood? At Bernice Worden's store? It seemed impossible. But Sheriff Schley had known Frank Worden for years—he wasn't the type to panic or exaggerate.

Within minutes, Schley was standing inside the familiar confines of Worden's Hardware, but tonight it felt different. The comfortable atmosphere of the neighborhood store had been replaced by something cold and ominous. Behind the counter, dark stains marked the wooden floor, and the large brass cash register that normally dominated the space was nowhere to be found.

."Last entry in the sales book shows 9:30 this morning," Frank explained, his voice carefully controlled. "Antifreeze. But there's no customer copy, and the register's gone."
Sheriff Schley followed the beam of his flashlight as it revealed droplets of blood leading from behind the counter, through the store, and out the back door. Someone tried to clean up, but the evidence remained clear. Whatever had happened here, Bernice Worden hadn't simply decided to close early and go home.
As investigators would later piece together, the timeline was devastatingly simple: Ed Gein had entered the store at 9:30 AM, ostensibly to purchase antifreeze. But what transpired during those few minutes would transform a routine business transaction into something unspeakable.

The question that would haunt investigators wasn't just what happened to Bernice Worden—it was what had driven a man known throughout the community as odd but harmless to commit an act of violence that seemed completely out of character.

The answer to that question lay waiting in a ramshackle farmhouse two miles outside town, where Ed Gein had been living alone since his mother's death twelve years earlier. What Sheriff Schley and his deputies would discover there would reveal that their quiet, eccentric neighbor had been harboring secrets that defied comprehension.
But first, they had to find him.

Chapter 2:
The House of Horrors

November 16, 1957 - 8:45 PM

Sheriff Art Schley thought he had seen the worst of what Ed Gein was capable of when he discovered Bernice Worden's mutilated corpse hanging in the summer kitchen. He was wrong.

As additional officers arrived at the Gein farmhouse and portable floodlights illuminated the property, the true scope of the nightmare they were dealing with began to emerge. What they would find inside the main house would challenge every assumption they'd ever made about human nature and leave several seasoned investigators requiring psychiatric care.

Deputy Peck was the first to enter the farmhouse, his flashlight beam cutting through the musty darkness of rooms that hadn't been properly cleaned in over a decade. The smell hit him immediately — a mixture of decay, unwashed laundry, and something else he couldn't quite identify but that made his stomach churn.

"Jesus, Mary, and Joseph," he whispered, his voice echoing in the cluttered interior.

The house was a maze of accumulated junk. Newspapers and magazines were stacked floor to ceiling in some rooms. Old clothing was piled in corners, mixed with farm tools, broken furniture, and household items that looked like they hadn't been disturbed since the 1940s. But it was what was mixed in with the ordinary debris that made this place extraordinary in the most horrific way imaginable.

On a kitchen table, investigators found a human skull that had been converted into a soup bowl. The top had been sawed off with surgical precision, and the interior had been cleaned and polished. Nearby sat four chairs, their seats replaced with strips of human skin that had been carefully tanned and stretched over the wooden frames.
In what had once been the living room, Deputy Martinez discovered a lampshade made from a human face. The skin had been preserved with the facial features intact—lips, nose, and even eyelashes still clearly visible. The electric cord ran through the mouth, giving the grotesque creation a ghoulish smile. "Schley, you need to see this," Martinez called out, his voice barely under control.

The sheriff made his way through the cluttered house to where Martinez stood frozen in the doorway of what appeared to be a bedroom. Inside, hanging on the walls like hunting trophies, were ten human skulls. Some still had hair attached, others had been completely cleaned.

Several showed evidence of having been modified holes drilled for hanging, or the tops sawed off to create bowls.
But perhaps most disturbing of all was what they found in a paper bag sitting on a cluttered dresser: the preserved heads of two women, wrapped in brown paper like groceries from the local market.

As the investigation continued through the night, the catalog of horrors grew longer. They found belts made from human skin, complete with nipples still attached. There were nine masks crafted from the faces of women, each one carefully preserved and showing evidence of being worn. In a shoebox under a bed, investigators discovered a collection of human noses.

The kitchen yielded its own nightmares. In addition to the skull bowls, they found human bone fragments mixed in with animal bones, as if Gein had been making some kind of grotesque soup. Refrigerated in an old icebox were several human organs, including what appeared to be a human heart wrapped in butcher paper.

Perhaps most chilling was the discovery of what investigators would later learn was a "woman suit"—a complete vest made from the torso of a female victim, including breasts and female genitalia. The suit had been carefully crafted, with string ties that would allow someone to wear it like a macabre costume.

"How long has this been going on?" Deputy Peck asked Sheriff Schley as they stood in the kitchen, surrounded by evidence of horrors that defied comprehension.

Schley didn't have an answer. Based on the number of remains they were finding, it was clear that Ed Gein had been collecting human body parts for years, possibly more than a decade. But where had all these people come from? Plainfield was a small community—if this many people had gone missing, surely someone would have noticed.

The answer to that question would emerge over the following days as investigators began the grim task of trying to identify the remains. What they discovered would reveal that Ed Gein had been operating as both a murderer and a grave robber, stealing recently buried bodies from local cemeteries to fuel his macabre hobby.

November 17, 1957 - 6:00 AM

Word of the discovery at the Gein farm spread through Plainfield like wildfire, despite law enforcement's attempts to control information. By dawn, reporters from Milwaukee and Madison newspapers were descending on the small farming community, followed shortly by radio and television crews from as far away as Chicago.

The residents of Plainfield woke up to find their quiet town transformed into a media circus. Camera crews set up outside the courthouse, reporters interviewed anyone willing to talk, and curious onlookers began arriving from across the state to get a glimpse of the house where such unthinkable horrors had taken place.

For the people who had known Ed Gein all their lives, the revelations were almost impossible to process. This was the same man who had helped neighbors with their farm work, who had babysat local children, who had seemed harmless if eccentric. How could someone who appeared so normal on the surface have been capable of such monstrous acts?

Mrs. Hill, whose husband Henry had provided Gein with an alibi for the day of Bernice Worden's disappearance, was among the most shaken. "He seemed like such a gentle soul," she told reporters gathered on her front porch. "He was always polite, always helpful. I can't believe... I just can't believe it."

But as investigators continued their work at the farmhouse and began interviewing Gein in custody, a clearer picture began to emerge of the man behind the horrors. This wasn't a case of sudden psychotic break or temporary insanity. The evidence suggested years of careful planning, methodical execution, and a level of skill in preserving human remains that spoke to extensive practice.

12 Years Earlier - December 29, 1945

To understand how Ed Gein became the monster they arrested that November night, investigators would need to look back to the event that many would later identify as the turning point in his psychological development: the death of his mother, Augusta Gein.

Augusta Wilhelmina Gein had been the dominating force in her son's life from the moment of his birth on August 27, 1906. A fanatically religious woman with rigid moral views and an iron will, she had shaped every aspect of Ed's existence according to her own twisted vision of righteousness.

The Gein family had never been particularly social, but under Augusta's influence, they became increasingly isolated from their neighbors. She viewed the outside world as corrupt and dangerous, filled with temptations that could lead her sons astray. She was particularly suspicious of women, whom she saw as instruments of the devil designed to lure men into sin. "All women are whores except for me," Augusta would tell her sons repeatedly. "They're vessels of sin and corruption. You must never trust them, never let them into your heart."

Ed's father, George, was a weak man who had little influence in the household. An alcoholic who spent most of his time either working or drinking, he provided no counterbalance to Augusta's extreme views. When he died in 1940, Ed and his older brother Henry were left completely under their mother's psychological control.

Henry, who was several years older than Ed, had begun to question their mother's teachings as he reached adulthood. He would occasionally suggest that Augusta's views were extreme, that perhaps they should have more contact with their neighbors, that her constant criticism and control were unhealthy.

These suggestions infuriated Augusta and worried Ed, who couldn't imagine life without his mother's guidance. When Henry died in 1944 under mysterious circumstances—officially ruled an accident, though some investigators would later suspect that Ed might have been involved— Ed was left alone with the woman who had controlled every aspect of his existence.

For Ed, his mother wasn't just a parent—she was his entire world. She made every decision, controlled every aspect of his daily routine, and provided the only human contact he was allowed to have. When she suffered her first stroke in early 1945, Ed was devastated. When she died on December 29, 1945, following a series of additional strokes, his world collapsed entirely.

At age thirty-nine, Ed Gein found himself completely alone for the first time in his life. He had never learned to make independent decisions, never developed normal social relationships, never been allowed to think for himself. His mother had been his anchor, his guide, his reason for existing. Without her, he was psychologically adrift.

In the months following Augusta's death, Ed began to exhibit increasingly bizarre behavior. He sealed off most of the farmhouse, living only in a small section that he kept exactly as his mother had left it. He would spend hours in her bedroom, going through her possessions and talking to her as if she were still alive.

It was during this period that Ed began his nocturnal visits to local cemeteries. Initially, he would later claim, he was drawn there by curiosity about what death looked like, what happened to bodies after burial. But what started as morbid curiosity quickly escalated into something far more disturbing.

Ed began digging up recently buried bodies, particularly those of women who resembled his mother. He would bring parts of these corpses back to the farmhouse, where he would experiment with preserving and modifying them. What had started as an attempt to understand death became an obsession with creating new life from dead tissue.

Investigators would later theorize that Ed's grave robbing was initially an attempt to somehow bring his mother back, or at least to maintain some connection to her through contact with death. But over time, his activities became more elaborate and more disturbing.

He began creating household items from human remains — the skull bowls, the skin lampshades, the furniture upholstered with human skin. He told investigators that he had been trying to create a "woman suit" that would allow him to literally become a woman, to somehow transform himself into his mother.

But grave robbing, disturbing as it was, eventually wasn't enough to satisfy whatever psychological need drove Ed's behavior. The bodies he retrieved from cemeteries were often in advanced stages of decay, making them difficult to work with. He needed fresher material.
It was this need that led Ed to commit his first murder.

December 8, 1954 - Hogan's Tavern

Mary Hogan was a fifty-one-year-old divorcee who owned and operated a small tavern about six miles from the Gein farm. She was known throughout the area as a tough, independent woman who could handle rowdy customers and wasn't afraid to speak her mind. She also bore a physical resemblance to Augusta Gein — a fact that would prove tragically significant.

On the snowy evening of December 8, 1954, Mary was working alone at the tavern when Ed Gein walked in. What happened next would remain largely a mystery, as Ed's accounts of the evening would vary significantly in the years that followed. But the basic facts were clear: Ed shot Mary Hogan in the head with a .32 caliber revolver, loaded her body into his pickup truck, and drove back to his farmhouse. Unlike the grave-robbed bodies he had been working with, Mary Hogan's corpse was fresh and intact. This allowed Ed to experiment with preservation techniques he had been developing, and to create the kinds of items that would later horrify investigators at the farmhouse.

Mary Hogan's disappearance caused considerable concern in the local community. Her car was found parked outside the tavern, the front door was standing open, and there were signs of a struggle inside. But with no body and no witnesses, investigators had little to work with. The case eventually went cold, though local residents continued to speculate about what might have happened to the tough tavern owner.

Ed, meanwhile, returned to his grave-robbing activities, supplemented now by the knowledge that murder could provide him with the fresher materials he needed for his increasingly elaborate projects. For nearly three years, he continued his nocturnal activities, robbing graves and occasionally committing murders when the opportunity arose. It was during this period that he created most of the horrific items investigators would later find in his house: the lampshades, the bowls, the furniture, and the woman suit that represented his ultimate goal of transformation.

November 16, 1957 - Present Day

As investigators continued their work at the Gein farmhouse, the full scope of his activities began to emerge. In addition to the remains found inside the house, they discovered evidence of multiple grave robberies at local cemeteries. At least nine graves had been disturbed, their occupants removed and taken back to the farm for Ed's experiments.

The bodies had been chosen according to specific criteria—all were women, most were middle aged, and many bore some physical resemblance to Augusta Gein. Ed had been attempting to recreate his mother through his macabre collection, to somehow bring her back to life through contact with death.

But perhaps most disturbing was the psychological profile that began to emerge from interviews with Ed himself. Far from the raving lunatic that many expected, Ed appeared calm, almost childlike in his explanations of what he had done. He spoke about his activities as if they were perfectly normal hobbies, showing no apparent understanding of why others found them horrifying.

"I just wanted to see what they looked like," he told investigators when asked about his graverobbing activities. "I was curious about death, about what happens to people after they die."

When pressed about the household items he had created from human remains, Ed's responses were equally matter-of-fact. "I needed those things. The house felt empty after Mother died. I was just trying to make it feel more like home."

It was clear to the investigators that Ed Gein was not a typical criminal. His crimes weren't motivated by anger, greed, or sexual gratification in any conventional sense. Instead, they seemed to spring from a profound psychological disturbance that had its roots in his relationship with his domineering mother and his complete inability to function as an independent adult.

Dr. Edward Kelley, the psychiatrist brought in to evaluate Ed, would later write: "The subject appears to suffer from a severe dissociative disorder, combined with elements of schizophrenia and what might be termed 'maternal fixation syndrome.' His crimes represent an attempt to literally merge with his deceased mother through contact with death and the creation of surrogate maternal figures from human remains." But for the residents of Plainfield, psychological explanations provided little comfort. Their quiet farming community had become forever associated with some of the most disturbing crimes in American history. The man they had known as an odd but harmless neighbor had been revealed as a monster whose activities defied comprehension.

As news of the discoveries at the Gein farm spread across the nation, it would inspire countless books, movies, and television shows. Characters like Norman Bates, Leatherface, and Buffalo Bill would all trace their origins back to the quiet bachelor farmer who had shocked the world with his unthinkable crimes.

But for those who had lived through the actual events, who had known Ed Gein personally and discovered the horrors he had been hiding, the reality was far more disturbing than any work of fiction could ever be.

The monster had been living among them all along, hiding behind a mask of rural politeness and helping neighbors with their chores. And if Ed Gein could fool an entire community for so many years, it raised a terrifying question that would haunt Plainfield for generations to come:

Chapter 3:

Mother's Boy

August 27, 1906 - La Crosse County, Wisconsin

The baby who would grow up to become America's most notorious grave robber entered the world during a violent thunderstorm that seemed to shake the very foundations of the small farmhouse where Augusta Gein labored to bring her second son into existence. As lightning illuminated the prairie sky and rain lashed against the windows, Edward Theodore Gein drew his first breath in a world that his mother had already decided was too corrupt and dangerous for innocent souls.

Augusta held her newborn son close, studying his features in the flickering lamplight. Unlike his older brother Henry, who had been a robust, healthy baby, little Eddie was small and delicate, with pale skin and fine features that reminded Augusta more of herself than of her husband George. This child, she decided, would need special protection from the evils that lurked beyond their farmhouse walls.

From his earliest moments, Ed Gein's life would be defined by his mother's obsessive need to control and protect him from what she saw as a world filled with sin and temptation. Augusta Gein was a woman whose religious fervor bordered on fanaticism, whose moral rigidity had hardened into something that resembled righteousness but was actually a form of psychological imprisonment for her family.

The Gein family farm sat on 160 acres of marginal land outside the small community of Plainfield. It was isolated even by rural Wisconsin standards, accessible only by a narrow dirt road that became nearly impassable during the spring thaw and winter storms. This isolation suited Augusta perfectly — the farther her family was from outside influences, the better she could protect them from corruption.

George Gein, Ed's father, was a weak man who had long ago surrendered any attempt to challenge his wife's iron will. An alcoholic who spent most of his time either working in the fields or drinking in town, George provided little more than financial support for the family. When he was home, he was usually either drunk or sleeping off the effects of his latest binge. The responsibility for raising the children fell entirely to Augusta, a burden she embraced with the fervor of a religious crusade.

"The world is full of evil, Eddie," Augusta would tell her younger son as she tucked him into bed each night. "Bad people who want to hurt good children like you. That's why you must always stay close to Mother. I'm the only one who truly loves you, the only one who will keep you safe."

As Ed grew from infant to toddler, Augusta's protective instincts became increasingly extreme. She forbade him from playing with other children, claiming they would teach him bad habits and lead him into sin. She monitored his every movement, his every word, his every thought. Nothing he did escaped her attention, and nothing he wanted mattered if it conflicted with her vision of what was best for him.

The only companion Ed was allowed was his older brother Henry, who at four years old was already showing signs of independence that worried their mother. Henry was more robust than Ed, more willing to question Augusta's rules, and more interested in the world beyond the farm. These traits made him both a source of fascination and concern for his younger brother.

"Henry thinks he knows better than Mother," Augusta would tell Ed when the older boy was out of earshot. "But he doesn't understand how dangerous the world really is. You're smarter than Henry, Eddie. You understand that Mother knows what's best."

Ed did understand, or at least he learned to act as if he did. From an early age, he discovered that agreeing with his mother, accepting her judgments without question, and demonstrating complete dependence on her guidance was the path to peace in the Gein household. Any attempt at independence was met with lectures about the dangers that awaited disobedient children, stories of what happened to boys who didn't listen to their mothers.

1912 - The Plainfield Schoolhouse

When Ed turned six, Wisconsin state law required that he begin attending school, a development that filled Augusta with dread. For six years, she had been able to control every aspect of her son's environment, to filter every influence that might shape his developing mind. Now she would be forced to send him into what she saw as a den of corruption and moral decay.

The Plainfield schoolhouse was a typical one-room rural school, serving children from kindergarten through eighth grade under the guidance of a single teacher. For most farm children, it represented their first real contact with the world beyond their families, a chance to form friendships and learn social skills that would serve them throughout their lives. For Ed Gein, it became a daily ordeal that reinforced every warning his mother had given him about the dangers of the outside world.

From his first day of school, Ed was different from the other children, and they knew it. While his classmates ran and played during recess, Ed sat quietly by himself, too nervous to join in their games. When the teacher called on him to answer questions, he would stutter and blush, his voice barely audible even in the small classroom.

The other children quickly identified Ed as an easy target for teasing and bullying. His clothes were old-fashioned and ill-fitting, his hair was cut in a style that looked like his mother had done it herself (which she had), and his pale, delicate features made him look younger than his actual age. Most damaging of all was his obvious fear of any situation that required him to act independently or make decisions without his mother's guidance.

"Eddie's a mama's boy," the other children would chant when the teacher wasn't listening.

"Eddie's afraid of his own shadow. Eddie can't do anything without asking his mommy first."

The taunting was cruel but accurate. Ed had never learned to function without his mother's constant supervision and approval. When faced with even simple decisions—which book to choose for reading time, whether to ask for help with a difficult problem—he would freeze with anxiety, paralyzed by the fear of making the wrong choice.

Miss Henderson, the schoolteacher, tried her best to help Ed adjust to the classroom environment. She was a kind woman who had taught farm children for nearly twenty years, and she recognized the signs of a child who was being overprotected at home. She made gentle attempts to draw Ed into group activities, to encourage him to make friends with his classmates.

But every effort was undermined by Augusta's influence at home. Each evening, she would interrogate Ed about his day at school, demanding to know what he had learned, who he had talked to, what the other children had said and done. When Ed mentioned any attempt by Miss Henderson to encourage his independence, Augusta would respond with lectures about the teacher's misguided intentions.

"She doesn't understand you like Mother does," Augusta would tell him. "She wants to fill your head with ideas that will lead you astray. You mustn't listen to her when she tells you to be more like the other children. The other children are bad, Eddie. They come from families that don't understand right from wrong."

Augusta's distrust of the school extended to the other students and their families. She viewed them all as potential corrupting influences on her son, sources of moral contamination that could undo years of careful training. When Ed mentioned classmates by name, she would find fault with their families — their fathers drank too much, their mothers were loose women, their homes were sites of sin and degradation.

"You must never forget that you're different from those children," Augusta would remind him nightly. "You come from a good family, a godly family. We have standards that others don't understand. That's why they don't like you, Eddie. It's not because there's anything wrong with you — it's because you're better than them, and they know it."

This constant reinforcement of Ed's supposed superiority, combined with his obvious social failures, created a complex psychological dynamic that would shape his personality for the rest of his life. He simultaneously believed himself to be special and chosen, while also feeling inadequate and fearful in any social situation.

The other children's rejection of Ed only confirmed Augusta's teachings about the corrupt nature of the outside world. Every taunt, every exclusion from games, every moment of loneliness at recess became evidence that her warnings had been correct. The world beyond the farm was indeed dangerous and hostile, filled with people who meant harm to innocent children like her Eddie.

1915 - The Death of Innocence

By the time Ed reached fourth grade, his social isolation at school had become complete. The other children had long since given up any attempts to include him in their activities, and he had learned to accept his role as the classroom outcast. He spent recess periods alone, lunch hours by himself, and walked to and from school without companions.

It was during this period that Ed first began to display the obsessive behaviors that would later characterize his adult life. He would spend hours arranging and rearranging his few possessions — his school books, his clothes, the small collection of rocks and leaves he kept in his bedroom. Everything had to be placed in exactly the right position, according to patterns and systems that made sense only to him.

Augusta encouraged these behaviors, seeing them as evidence of her son's superior intelligence and moral character. "You're naturally orderly, Eddie," she would tell him. "That's because you have a pure mind, uncoupled by the chaos that surrounds other children. God rewards those who maintain proper discipline."

But Ed's obsessive tendencies extended beyond simple orderliness. He began to develop elaborate rituals around everyday activities — specific ways of getting dressed, particular patterns for eating his meals, complex procedures for completing his school assignments. Any deviation from these rituals caused him intense anxiety, as if breaking his own rules might somehow invite the chaos that his mother had warned him about.

At school, Miss Henderson watched Ed's increasing withdrawal with growing concern. She had seen shy children before, children from overprotective families who took time to adjust to the classroom environment. But Ed's case was different. Instead of gradually adapting to social interaction, he seemed to be retreating further into himself with each passing month.

She made several attempts to speak with Augusta about Ed's social development, suggesting that perhaps he might benefit from more interaction with children his own age. These conversations were polite but unproductive. Augusta listened to the teacher's concerns with apparent attention, nodding and smiling, but it was clear that she had no intention of changing her approach to raising her son.

"Eddie is a sensitive child," Augusta would explain. "He needs more protection than other children, more guidance. He's not ready for the kind of independence you're suggesting, Miss Henderson. Perhaps when he's older, when his character is more firmly established."

But Miss Henderson suspected that Augusta had no intention of ever allowing Ed the independence that other children took for granted. She could see the psychological damage that such extreme protection was causing, but as a rural schoolteacher in 1915, she had limited ability to intervene in family matters.

The situation became even more troubling when Ed began to display signs of what would now be recognized as severe social anxiety disorder. He would sometimes become physically ill before school, vomiting or developing mysterious stomach pains that would disappear as soon as Augusta decided he was too sick to attend classes. These episodes became more frequent as the school year progressed, allowing Ed to spend more time at home under his mother's protective supervision.

Augusta saw these illnesses as confirmation that school was harmful to her son's delicate constitution. "Your body is telling you that school is not good for you, Eddie," she would say as she tucked him into bed on days when he was "too sick" to attend classes. "You're too pure, too sensitive for that rough environment. Mother will teach you what you need to know." And teach him she did, but the lessons had little to do with reading, writing, and arithmetic. Instead, Augusta used these home tutoring sessions to reinforce her worldview, to strengthen the psychological chains that bound her son to her side. She read to him from the Bible, focusing on passages about the corruption of the world and the need for the righteous to separate themselves from sinful influences.

"Remember the story of Lot's wife, Eddie," Augusta would say, referring to the Biblical figure who was turned into a pillar of salt for looking back at the destruction of Sodom and Gomorrah. "She couldn't resist the temptation to look back at the sinful world she was leaving behind, and God punished her for it. That's what happens to people who can't turn their backs on corruption— they become corrupted themselves."

The message was clear: any attraction to the world beyond the farm, any curiosity about normal social interaction, any desire for independence was a form of spiritual corruption that would inevitably lead to destruction. Ed learned to suppress such feelings, to see them as weaknesses that needed to be overcome rather than natural developmental impulses that should be encouraged.

1918 - The Great War and Greater Isolation

When America entered World War I, the conflict seemed very distant from the isolated Gein farm. But the war had indirect effects that would further shape Ed's unusual upbringing. Able-bodied men from the community were drafted into military service, leaving farms understaffed and creating economic uncertainty that affected even the most isolated families.

George Gein, now in his late thirties and with a family to support, was too old for the draft. But the war created new pressures on the farm as demand for agricultural products increased while labor became scarce. He was forced to work longer hours, leaving Augusta even more solely responsible for the children's upbringing.

Henry, now sixteen, had grown into a strong, capable young man who was increasingly valuable as a farm laborer. But his years of questioning his mother's extreme views had created a source of tension in the household that was becoming harder to ignore. He would openly challenge Augusta's restrictions, arguing that Ed needed more contact with the outside world, more opportunities to develop normal social skills.

"He's twelve years old, Ma," Henry would say during family discussions about Ed's education and social development. "He should be making friends, learning to get along with other kids. You're going to cripple him if you keep him tied to your apron strings like this."

These challenges to her authority infuriated Augusta and worried Ed, who had learned to see any criticism of his mother as a personal attack on the foundation of his world. When Henry suggested that Augusta's methods might be wrong, Ed felt as if the ground beneath his feet was shifting, as if the one stable element in his universe was being threatened.

"Henry doesn't understand us, Eddie," Augusta would tell her younger son after these confrontations. "He's been influenced by the crude thinking of the men he works with in the fields. He's starting to think like his father, and you know how that ends—with drinking and laziness and moral decay."

The comparison to George was a particularly cutting criticism in Augusta's lexicon. She viewed her husband as a weak man who had been corrupted by worldly influences, who had chosen alcohol and self-indulgence over moral discipline and family responsibility. The suggestion that Henry was following the same path was tantamount to predicting his spiritual doom.

For Ed, these family conflicts created intense psychological pressure. He loved his older brother and looked up to him in many ways, but he was also completely dependent on his mother's approval and guidance. When forced to choose between Henry's suggestions for greater independence and Augusta's demands for continued dependence, Ed invariably chose his mother's side.

"Mother knows what's best for me," he would tell Henry when pressed to assert himself. "She's kept me safe all these years. Why would I stop listening to her now?"
But privately, Ed was beginning to experience the first stirrings of adolescent curiosity about the world beyond the farm. At twelve, his body was beginning to change, and with it came new thoughts and feelings that his mother's teachings couldn't fully explain or suppress. He found himself wondering what it would be like to have friends, to go places without his mother's supervision, to make decisions based on his own desires rather than her approval.

These thoughts terrified him almost as much as they intrigued him. Augusta had taught him that such feelings were dangerous, that they represented the first steps toward the kind of moral corruption that had destroyed so many other families. When he experienced curiosity about girls, interest in activities his mother disapproved of, or simple desires for independence, he would feel overwhelmed with guilt and anxiety.

The solution he developed was to confess these feelings to his mother, to expose every wayward thought and seek her guidance in overcoming what he had been taught to see as temptation. These confession sessions became a regular part of Ed's routine, reinforcing Augusta's control while simultaneously intensifying his psychological dependence on her approval.

"I'm glad you told me about these thoughts, Eddie," Augusta would say after these sessions. "It shows that your conscience is working properly, that you understand the difference between right and wrong. Many boys your age give in to these temptations without even realizing they're doing wrong. But you're stronger than that. You have Mother to help you resist."

These confession sessions served multiple purposes for Augusta. They gave her detailed intelligence about her son's psychological state, allowing her to identify and address any signs of independence before they could develop into serious challenges to her authority. They also reinforced Ed's belief that he was incapable of managing his own moral and emotional life without her guidance.

Most importantly, they created a psychological dynamic in which Ed's natural developmental impulses were redefined as moral failings that required constant vigilance and maternal supervision to overcome. Instead of learning to trust his own judgment and develop his own moral compass, Ed learned to see his independent thoughts and feelings as evidence of his fundamental weakness and corruption.

1920 - The End of Education

When Ed completed eighth grade at the age of fourteen, Augusta made the decision that would seal his fate as a lifelong dependent. Instead of allowing him to continue his education at the high school in town, she declared that his formal schooling was complete and that he would remain on the farm to help with the family's agricultural operations.

This decision was not unusual for farm children in rural Wisconsin during the 1920s. Many families needed their children's labor to maintain their agricultural operations, and high school was often seen as an unnecessary luxury that interfered with practical training in farming skills. But for Ed, who was already severely isolated and psychologically dependent, the end of his formal education represented the closing of his last connection to the normal world.

"High school would be a waste of time for you, Eddie," Augusta explained. "You'd be exposed to all sorts of corrupt influences—older children who use foul language, teachers who don't understand proper moral values, ideas that contradict everything Mother has taught you. Why risk all that when you can learn everything you really need to know right here on the farm?"

The decision also served Augusta's deeper psychological needs. With Ed working alongside her every day, she could maintain the level of supervision and control that had defined their relationship since his birth. She could monitor his every action, guide his every decision, and ensure that no outside influences could challenge the worldview she had so carefully constructed.

For Ed, the end of school represented both relief and loss. He was genuinely glad to escape the daily humiliation of his social isolation, the constant reminder that he was different from other children in ways that made him unacceptable to his peers. But he also lost his last opportunity to develop the social skills and independent thinking abilities that might have allowed him to eventually break free from his mother's psychological domination.

Henry, now eighteen and increasingly independent, watched these developments with growing alarm. He could see that his younger brother was being deliberately crippled, prevented from developing the tools he would need to function as an independent adult. But Henry's attempts to intervene were met with fierce resistance from both Augusta and Ed himself.

"You're trying to destroy our family," Augusta would accuse Henry when he suggested that Ed needed more independence. "You want to fill Eddie's head with the same corrupt ideas that have ruined you. Well, I won't let that happen. Eddie is a good boy, and he's going to stay that way." Ed, caught between his brother's concern and his mother's anger, invariably sided with Augusta. By this point in his development, the psychological bonds that tied him to his mother were so strong that he literally could not imagine life without her constant guidance and approval. The suggestion that he might be better off with more independence felt like a threat to his very survival.

"I don't want to leave Mother," he would tell Henry. "She needs me here, and I need her. Why can't you understand that we're happy the way we are?"

But happiness was perhaps too strong a word for what Ed experienced in his relationship with Augusta. It was more accurate to say that he had achieved a kind of psychological equilibrium in which his complete dependence on his mother provided him with the security he craved, while her total control over his life eliminated the anxiety he felt when forced to make independent decisions.

This equilibrium came at an enormous cost. At fourteen, Ed had the emotional and social development of a much younger child. He had never learned to form relationships with peers, never experienced the kind of independence that allows children to develop confidence in their own judgment, never had the opportunity to discover his own interests and abilities separate from his mother's expectations.

Most tragically, he had internalized Augusta's view of the world as a fundamentally dangerous and corrupt place where only complete dependence on her protection could ensure his safety and moral purity. This worldview would shape every aspect of his adult life, creating the psychological foundation for the horrors that would eventually emerge from the isolated farmhouse where Augusta Gein ruled with absolute authority over her increasingly disturbed son.

As Ed entered adolescence under his mother's intensified supervision, the stage was being set for a psychological drama that would play out over the next twenty-five years. The boy who had been too frightened to play with classmates, too dependent to make simple decisions, too isolated to develop normal social skills, was evolving into something that defied easy categorization.

He was becoming Augusta Gein's perfect creation: a son so completely dependent on her guidance that he literally could not exist without her. The question that would haunt investigators decades later was what would happen to such a person when the source of his psychological stability was suddenly removed.

The answer to that question lay waiting in the future, in a cold winter night when Augusta Gein would finally release her grip on her son's soul, leaving behind a man who had never learned to be human on his own terms.
To be continued...

Chapter 4:
Brothers in Shadow

May 16, 1944 - The Gein Farm

The fire started in the marsh grass behind the Gein farmhouse just after two o'clock on a warm spring afternoon. Henry Gein, now thirty-seven years old and the stronger of Augusta's two sons, had been burning brush when the flames got away from him, spreading quickly through the dry vegetation that surrounded the isolated property.

By the time neighbors spotted the smoke and arrived to help fight the blaze, both Henry and his younger brother Ed were working frantically to contain the fire before it could reach the farm buildings. The two men made an odd pair — Henry tall and robust, moving with the confident efficiency of someone accustomed to hard physical labor, while Ed remained thin and pale, his movements nervous and uncertain even in the face of genuine emergency.

What happened next would become the subject of speculation and whispered conversations in Plainfield for years to come. When the fire was finally extinguished and the volunteers began heading home, Henry Gein was nowhere to be found.

Ed, his face streaked with soot and his hands shaking from exhaustion, told the assembled firefighters that he had lost track of his brother during the confusion of fighting the blaze. Henry had been working in a different section of the marsh, Ed explained, and when the smoke cleared, he was simply gone.

"I called and called for him," Ed told Sheriff Schley, who had arrived to assess the situation. "But the smoke was so thick, and the fire was moving so fast. I don't know where he could have gone."

A search party was organized immediately. Two dozen men spread out across the burned marshland, calling Henry's name and examining every blackened patch of ground where a man might have fallen overcome by smoke. The search continued until well after dark, with lanterns and flashlights casting eerie shadows across the scorched landscape.
It was Ed who found his brother's body.

Henry was lying in a small clearing approximately a quarter mile from where the fire had started, his body positioned in a way that suggested he had simply laid down and never gotten up again. His clothes were barely singed, and there were no signs that he had been burned by the flames. The official cause of death was listed as asphyxiation from smoke inhalation, though the coroner noted that the body showed no evidence of the kind of smoke damage typically associated with such deaths.

More puzzling were the bruises found on Henry's head—injuries that could have resulted from a fall, but which some observers thought looked more like the result of blunt force trauma. Dr. Morrison, the county coroner, mentioned these injuries in his report but concluded that they were consistent with Henry having collapsed and struck his head on a rock during the fire.

No one questioned Ed's account of events. No one suggested that there might be more to Henry's death than a tragic accident during a brush fire. No one wondered why the younger, weaker brother had managed to survive an ordeal that had killed his older, stronger sibling. No one except Augusta Gein, who watched her surviving son during the funeral service with eyes that revealed nothing of what she might be thinking.

1921-1940 - The Years of Growing Tension

To understand what might have happened in that marsh on May 16, 1944, it's necessary to examine the nineteen years that preceded Henry's death—years during which the relationship between Augusta's two sons had evolved from childhood companionship into something far more complex and dangerous.

After Ed left school in 1920, the dynamic within the Gein household began to shift in ways that created increasing psychological pressure on all its members. Henry, now in his early twenties, was reaching the age when most young men would be expected to leave home, find work, perhaps start families of their own. But Augusta's iron grip on her sons' lives made such normal development impossible.

For Henry, who had always been more independent-minded than his younger brother, this restriction became increasingly unbearable. He could see what Augusta's overprotection was doing to Ed, how it was stunting his emotional and social development, turning him into something that wasn't quite a child but could never become a fully functioning adult.

"She's destroying him," Henry would tell his father during their rare private conversations. "Eddie's twenty years old, and he can't make a decision about what to have for breakfast without asking her permission. What's going to happen to him when she's gone?"

George Gein, now in his sixties and increasingly frail, had long since given up any attempt to challenge his wife's methods of child-rearing. His response to Henry's concerns was typically passive: "Your mother knows what she's doing. She's kept you boys safe and out of trouble all these years."

But Henry could see that safety and isolation were not the same thing as healthy development. Ed was becoming increasingly strange, his behavior more rigid and ritualistic with each passing year. He would spend hours arranging and rearranging objects in his room, following complex patterns that made sense only to him. He would have long conversations with himself, practicing responses to hypothetical social situations that he would never actually encounter given his mother's restrictions on contact with the outside world.

Most disturbing to Henry was the way Ed talked about their mother. There was a quality of worship in his voice when he spoke of Augusta, a reverence that went far beyond normal filial affection. Ed seemed to view his mother not just as a parent or authority figure, but as some kind of divine presence whose wisdom was absolute and whose approval was essential for his very survival.

"Mother understands things that other people don't," Ed would say when Henry tried to discuss the possibility of the brothers having more independence. "She can see dangers that we can't see. She knows what's best for us."
"Eddie, you're a grown man," Henry would respond. "You should be able to decide for yourself what's best. You should be thinking about getting married, having a family of your own, making your own decisions."

These conversations would invariably end with Ed becoming agitated and eventually confessing to Augusta that Henry had been trying to "put ideas in his head." Augusta's response was always swift and severe—lectures about Henry's corrupted thinking, warnings about the dangers of listening to anyone who questioned maternal authority, and renewed emphasis on the special bond between mother and son that no outside influence should be allowed to disturb.

"Henry has been influenced by the crude thinking of the men he works with," Augusta would tell Ed after these incidents. "He's starting to think like the worldly people in town, people who don't understand the importance of family loyalty and moral purity. You must not let him poison your mind with his modern ideas."

For Augusta, Henry's growing independence represented a fundamental threat to the psychological system she had constructed. If one son could successfully challenge her authority and establish an independent existence, it might encourage the other to do the same. And losing Ed—her favorite, her most devoted follower, the son who had never seriously questioned her absolute authority—was unthinkable.

The solution was to systematically undermine Henry's influence while strengthening Ed's dependence. Augusta began to assign the brothers different tasks, ensuring that they spent less time working together and more time under her direct supervision. She would schedule Ed's activities to conflict with times when Henry might have tried to talk with him privately. Most effectively, she began to share "confidential" information with Ed about Henry's supposed moral failings and character defects.

"I don't like to speak ill of family," Augusta would tell Ed, "but I'm worried about your brother. He's been asking questions about things that are none of his business, spending time with people who are a bad influence on him. I'm afraid he's losing his moral compass."

These conversations served multiple purposes. They reinforced Ed's belief that his mother possessed special insight into people's character. They created suspicion and distance between the brothers. Most importantly, they established a special bond between Augusta and Ed based on shared knowledge and mutual trust that explicitly excluded Henry.

Ed, who had been taught from birth to view his mother's judgments as infallible, accepted these characterizations of Henry without question. His brother's attempts to encourage independence began to seem less like helpful advice and more like evidence of moral corruption. When Henry suggested that Ed should think for himself, Ed began to hear this as temptation rather than guidance.

1940 - The Death of George Gein

The dynamic within the Gein household shifted dramatically when George Gein died of heart failure in April 1940. At sixty-six, he had been in declining health for several years, his body worn down by decades of hard farm labor and heavy drinking. His death, while not unexpected, removed the last buffer between Augusta's psychological control and her sons' daily lives.

For Henry, his father's death represented both loss and opportunity. George had been a weak man who had failed to protect his sons from their mother's psychological manipulation, but he had also been the only other adult in the household who might occasionally question Augusta's more extreme decisions. With George gone, Augusta's authority would be absolute and unchallenged.

But his father's death also meant that Henry, as the older son, would be expected to take over more responsibility for the farm's operations. This new role might provide him with the leverage he needed to finally assert some independence, to create space for both himself and Ed to develop more normal lives.

For Ed, his father's death was primarily significant because of how it affected his mother. Augusta had never shown much affection for her husband, but his death still represented a major change in the household structure that she had controlled for so many years. In the weeks following George's funeral, she became even more possessive of her surviving sons, even more determined to prevent any outside influences from disrupting the family unit she had worked so hard to create.

"Now it's just the three of us," she told Henry and Ed during a family meeting held shortly after George's burial. "We must stick together more than ever. The world is full of people who will try to take advantage of a widow and her sons, people who will try to break up our family for their own benefit. We cannot let that happen."

But Henry had reached the point where such appeals to family loyalty no longer carried the weight they once had. At thirty-three, he was well past the age when most men would have established independent lives. He had watched his younger brother's psychological development arrested at the level of a dependent child, and he had seen how his mother's control had prevented both sons from forming the kinds of relationships and experiences that might have allowed them to grow into functional adults.

"Ma, Eddie and I are grown men," Henry said during that family meeting. "We need to start making our own decisions, living our own lives. You can't keep us tied to your apron strings forever."

Augusta's response was swift and harsh. "Your father's death has obviously affected your thinking more than I realized," she said. "You're talking like a selfish person, someone who cares more about his own desires than about his family's welfare. I expected better from you, Henry."

But this time, Henry didn't back down. "It's not selfish to want a normal life, Ma. It's not selfish to think that Eddie should have a chance to meet people his own age, maybe find a wife, have children of his own. What you're doing to him isn't protection—it's imprisonment."

These words hit Augusta like a physical blow. For years, she had been able to control Henry's rebellious impulses through a combination of guilt, religious instruction, and appeals to family loyalty. But now he was directly challenging not just her decisions, but the fundamental philosophy that governed her approach to raising her sons.

The confrontation marked the beginning of an escalating conflict that would define the household dynamics for the next four years. Henry began to openly question Augusta's restrictions, to suggest alternative approaches to family life, to encourage Ed to think for himself. Augusta responded by intensifying her psychological pressure on both sons, but particularly on Ed, who remained her most reliable ally in the struggle for control of the family.

For Ed, this conflict created an impossible psychological situation. On one hand, he loved and respected his older brother, who had been his only companion and protector during their isolated childhood. On the other hand, he was completely dependent on his mother's approval and guidance, unable to imagine life without her constant supervision and control.

When forced to choose between Henry's suggestions for independence and Augusta's demands for continued dependence, Ed invariably chose his mother's side. But the choice was becoming more difficult with each confrontation, and the psychological stress of being caught between the two most important people in his life was beginning to show in increasingly disturbed behavior.

Ed began to exhibit signs of what would now be recognized as severe anxiety and obsessive-compulsive disorder. His ritualistic behaviors became more elaborate and time-consuming. He developed new phobias and superstitions that governed his daily activities. Most disturbing, he began to have what he described as "spells"—periods of disorientation during which he would lose track of time and find himself in locations with no memory of how he had gotten there.

Augusta interpreted these symptoms as evidence that Henry's influence was having a corrupting effect on Ed's naturally pure character. "You see what happens when you listen to your brother's ideas?" she would tell Ed after particularly severe episodes. "Your mind becomes confused because you're trying to serve two masters. You must choose between Mother's guidance and Henry's corruption. You cannot have both."

1941-1943 - The Final Conflict

The entry of the United States into World War II in December 1941 created new pressures within the Gein household that would ultimately prove fatal to the brothers' relationship. With thousands of young men being drafted into military service, there was increased demand for agricultural workers and growing social pressure on able-bodied men to contribute to the war effort either through military service or increased farm production.

Henry, at thirty-four, was too old for the draft, but he was still young enough to feel the social expectations that surrounded men of military age during wartime. He began to talk about the possibility of finding work in town, perhaps at one of the defense plants that were springing up across Wisconsin to support the war effort. For the first time, he had a socially acceptable reason to leave the farm and establish an independent life.

Augusta was horrified by this possibility. Losing Henry would be bad enough, but she also feared that his departure might encourage Ed to seek his own independence. The thought of being left alone on the farm, without either son to provide companionship and labor, was terrifying to a woman who had spent decades organizing her entire existence around controlling her children's lives.

"How can you even think about abandoning your family during such uncertain times?" Augusta demanded when Henry first mentioned the possibility of taking a job in town. "Your country needs farmers more than it needs factory workers. Your family needs you here, where you belong."

But Henry was no longer susceptible to such arguments. "My country needs men who are willing to serve however they can," he replied. "And my family needs to learn to function without being dependent on each other for everything. What's going to happen to Eddie if something happens to you, Ma? He can't even go to the grocery store by himself."

This observation struck at the heart of Augusta's deepest fears. She knew that Ed was psychologically incapable of independent living, that years of overprotection had left him unable to function without constant supervision and guidance. But rather than seeing this as evidence that her methods had been wrong, she interpreted it as proof that her protection was more necessary than ever.

"Eddie is a sensitive soul," Augusta would argue. "He needs more care and guidance than other people. That's not a weakness—it's a sign of his spiritual purity. The world is too corrupt for someone like Eddie to navigate alone. That's why God gave him a mother who understands his special needs." But Henry could see that what Augusta called "spiritual purity" was actually psychological damage. Ed's "sensitivity" was really an inability to cope with normal social interaction. His "special needs" were the result of deliberate psychological crippling that had prevented him from developing the skills necessary for independent living.

The conflict between the brothers intensified during 1942 and 1943, with Henry becoming increasingly direct in his criticism of Augusta's methods and Ed becoming increasingly agitated by the challenge to his mother's authority. Family meals became tense affairs, with long silences broken only by carefully worded exchanges that carried multiple layers of meaning.

"I saw the Johnson boy in town yesterday," Henry might say, referring to a local young man who had recently married. "He and his wife just bought a little house near the church. Seems like a nice setup for a young couple starting out." Augusta would respond immediately: "The Johnson boy always was too impulsive. Marriage is a serious responsibility that requires careful thought and proper guidance. Young people today rush into things without considering the consequences." Ed would remain silent during these exchanges, but Henry could see the effect they were having on his younger brother. Ed was beginning to show signs of serious psychological disturbance— periods of depression alternating with manic energy, increasingly elaborate compulsive behaviors, and a disturbing tendency to have long conversations with himself in which he seemed to be taking both sides of an internal argument.

Most alarming was the way Ed talked about their mother when she wasn't present. Henry began to notice that Ed's reverence for Augusta was taking on an almost religious quality, as if she were some kind of divine figure rather than a human parent with human flaws.

"Mother knows things that other people don't understand," Ed would say when Henry tried to discuss the possibility of both brothers establishing more independent lives. "She can see into people's hearts, see their true nature. She's warned me about the dangers of the outside world, and everything she's ever predicted has come true."

"Eddie, she's just a person," Henry would respond. "She's our mother, and we love her, but she's not infallible. She's kept us isolated here because she's afraid of losing control, not because the outside world is as dangerous as she claims." These conversations would invariably end with Ed becoming agitated and eventually reporting to Augusta that Henry had been "saying bad things" about her. Augusta's response was always to reinforce Ed's dependence while further undermining Henry's influence.

"Your brother is becoming like your father," Augusta would tell Ed after these incidents. "He's allowing worldly thinking to corrupt his judgment. He's lost sight of what's truly important—family loyalty, moral purity, the special bond between a mother and her devoted son."

By early 1944, the psychological pressure within the Gein household had reached a breaking point. Henry was openly planning to leave the farm, perhaps to take a job in Madison or Milwaukee where he could finally establish an independent life. Ed was showing signs of severe mental instability, caught between his love for his brother and his psychological dependence on his mother's approval.

Augusta, faced with the possibility of losing control over both sons, began to take increasingly desperate measures to maintain her authority. She started to share with Ed detailed accounts of Henry's supposed moral failings, stories about how his independence had led him to consort with "loose women" and "drinking companions" who were corrupting his character. "I hate to tell you this, Eddie," Augusta would say, "but I saw your brother talking to that Murphy girl from town. You know what kind of family the Murphys are—Irish Catholics with no moral standards whatsoever. I'm afraid Henry is being led astray by exactly the kind of people I've always warned you about."

These stories may have been fabrications, but they served their intended purpose of creating suspicion and resentment between the brothers. Ed, who had been taught to view his mother's judgments as absolute truth, began to see Henry's independence not as healthy development but as evidence of moral corruption. The stage was set for a confrontation that would resolve the conflict between the brothers in the most final way possible.

May 16, 1944 - The Day of Fire

The events of that spring afternoon began innocuously enough. Henry had been burning brush in the marshland behind the farmhouse, a routine activity that farmers throughout Wisconsin engaged in each spring to clear accumulated debris and prepare for the growing season. Ed had been helping, though his contributions were more hindrance than help given his nervous, inefficient approach to physical labor.

What happened next would be reconstructed years later by investigators who had begun to suspect that Henry Gein's death was not the accident it appeared to be. The official story — that Henry had been overcome by smoke while fighting a grass fire — never quite made sense to those who knew both brothers well. Henry was an experienced outdoorsman who had been burning brush for years without incident.

He was physically strong and capable, not the kind of person who would panic or become disoriented in a situation he had handled successfully dozens of times before. Most puzzling was the location where his body was found — in a small clearing that showed no evidence of fire damage, far from the area where the blaze had actually occurred.

The bruises on Henry's head, noted but not thoroughly investigated by the county coroner, suggested a different story. Medical experts who would later review the case files concluded that the injuries were consistent with blunt force trauma, possibly from a blow delivered with a heavy object like a shovel or piece of farm equipment.

More telling was Ed's behavior in the days following his brother's death. Instead of the grief and confusion that might be expected from someone who had lost his only sibling in a tragic accident, Ed seemed almost relieved. The psychological tension that had been building in the household for years was suddenly gone, replaced by a calm that some observers found disturbing. "He doesn't seem particularly broken up about losing Henry," neighbors would whisper to each other after the funeral. "You'd think he'd be more upset, losing his only brother like that." But for those who understood the psychological dynamics within the Gein household, Ed's reaction made perfect sense. Henry's death had resolved the impossible conflict that had been tearing Ed apart for years. No longer would he be forced to choose between his brother's suggestions for independence and his mother's demands for continued dependence. The source of doubt and confusion had been eliminated, leaving Ed free to embrace his psychological bondage to Augusta without internal conflict.

Augusta's reaction to Henry's death was more complex. Publicly, she played the role of grieving mother, accepting condolences from neighbors and maintaining the facade of a family tragedy. But those who knew her well could see that Henry's death had not been entirely unwelcome. The son who had challenged her authority, who had threatened to disrupt the psychological system she had spent decades constructing, was gone. The son who remained was completely devoted to her, incapable of independent thought or action, perfectly suited to be her eternal companion and protector.

In the weeks following Henry's funeral, Augusta and Ed settled into a new routine that would define the final year of Augusta's life. With Henry gone, there was no longer any challenge to Augusta's absolute authority over her surviving son. Ed's psychological development, which had been arrested at the level of a dependent child, became even more extreme. He began to exhibit behaviors that bordered on complete psychological merger with his mother—anticipating her needs before she expressed them, echoing her opinions on every subject, organizing his entire existence around her comfort and approval.

For Augusta, this represented the ultimate victory in her lifelong campaign to maintain control over her children. She had successfully eliminated the threat to her authority and retained the devotion of the son who mattered most to her. But this victory would prove to be temporary. In less than a year, Augusta herself would be dead, leaving behind a man who had never learned to exist as an independent human being.
The psychological time bomb that Augusta had created through years of extreme overprotection was about to explode, with consequences that would horrify the world and forever change how America understood the monsters that could be created through distorted family relationships.

But on that spring day in 1944, as Ed Gein stood over his brother's body in the marshland behind their farmhouse, he felt only relief. The voice that had urged him toward independence was finally silent. The person who had challenged his mother's wisdom was gone forever.

Now it was just Ed and Augusta, exactly as she had always wanted it to be. The question that remained was what would happen to such a psychologically damaged man when his source of stability and identity was suddenly removed. The answer to that question lay waiting in the darkness of December 29, 1945, when Augusta Gein would finally release her grip on her son's soul, leaving behind a creature that was no longer fully human.

Chapter 5:
The Death of Everything

December 29, 1945 - 3:17 AM

Augusta Gein died as she had lived—fighting for control until the very end. The massive stroke that would finally claim her life struck without warning in the early morning hours of December 29, 1945, but even as her body failed, she managed to call out for the one person who had never disappointed her, never challenged her authority, never questioned her absolute wisdom.

"Eddie," she gasped, her voice barely audible in the darkness of the farmhouse bedroom. "Eddie, come to Mother." Ed, who had been sleeping in the small room adjacent to his mother's—the same room he had occupied since childhood—woke instantly at the sound of her distress. At thirty-nine years old, he had never spent a single night away from the farmhouse, never made a major decision without his mother's guidance, never existed as anything other than an extension of Augusta's will and personality.

What he found when he rushed to her bedside would haunt him for the rest of his life. Augusta was conscious but clearly dying, her body partially paralyzed by the stroke, her speech slurred but her eyes still burning with the fierce intelligence that had dominated his existence for nearly four decades.

"Don't let them take me away from you, Eddie," she whispered as he knelt beside her bed. "Promise Mother you won't let them put me in the ground where I'll be cold and alone. Promise me you'll find a way to keep us together."
Ed's response was immediate and desperate: "I promise, Mother. I'll never let anyone separate us. You'll always be with me, no matter what happens."

Augusta smiled then, a expression of satisfaction that seemed almost peaceful despite the circumstances. She had spent thirty-nine years molding her younger son into the perfect dependent, the ideal companion who would never challenge her authority or seek independence from her control. Even in death, she was extracting promises that would ensure her continued influence over his life.

"You're a good boy, Eddie," she said, her voice growing fainter with each word. "You're Mother's special boy. Don't ever let anyone tell you different."

Those were Augusta Gein's last words. She died at 3:47 AM on December 29, 1945, leaving behind a son who had never learned to exist without her guidance, never developed the psychological tools necessary for independent living, never been allowed to discover who he might have been if given the chance to grow into a functional adult.

For Ed Gein, his mother's death represented the end of everything that had given his life meaning and structure. Augusta hadn't just been his parent—she had been his entire world, his source of identity, his anchor to reality itself. Without her constant presence and guidance, he was psychologically adrift in a way that few people could understand or imagine.

December 30, 1945 - The Day After

The twenty-four hours following Augusta's death revealed the full extent of Ed's psychological dependence on his mother. Neighbors who came to offer condolences and assistance found him in a state that went far beyond normal grief. He seemed completely unable to function, unable to make even the simplest decisions about funeral arrangements, unable to process the reality of what had happened.

"He just sat there staring at nothing," Mrs. Hill would later tell investigators. "I tried to talk to him about calling the funeral home, about notifying relatives, about all the things that need to be done when someone passes. But it was like he couldn't hear me, or couldn't understand what I was saying." Dr. Morrison, the county coroner who had been called to certify Augusta's death, was struck by Ed's unusual reaction to his mother's passing. While grief took many forms, and people processed loss differently, there was something disturbing about the way Ed seemed to have shut down completely in the face of his mother's death.

"Most people, even in the deepest grief, can still function on a basic level," Dr. Morrison would later recall. "They can answer questions, make simple decisions, go through the motions of daily life even when they're devastated emotionally. But Ed seemed to have lost the ability to do any of those things. It was as if his mother's death had severed some essential connection that allowed him to interact with the world."
The funeral arrangements were ultimately handled by neighbors and distant relatives, with Ed providing little input beyond nodding agreement to whatever decisions others made for him. He attended Augusta's burial service at the Plainfield Cemetery on January 2, 1946, standing silently beside the grave as the casket was lowered into the frozen ground.

But those who watched him carefully during the service noticed something disturbing about his behavior. Instead of the tears or emotional breakdown that might be expected from someone losing the most important person in their life, Ed seemed to be studying the burial process with an intensity that was almost clinical. He watched as the casket disappeared into the earth, observed how the grave was filled and marked, noted every detail of how the dead were committed to the ground. "He was memorizing it," one neighbor would later tell investigators. "Like he was taking notes on how the whole thing worked. It gave me the shivers, watching him watch them bury his mother like that."

January 1946 - The First Month Alone

In the weeks following Augusta's funeral, the full scope of Ed's psychological damage began to emerge. Neighbors who checked on him found that he had sealed off most of the farmhouse, living only in a small section that included the kitchen and his childhood bedroom. Augusta's room remained exactly as she had left it, her clothes still hanging in the closet, her personal belongings arranged precisely as they had been on the day she died.

Ed spent hours each day in his mother's room, sitting in her chair, going through her possessions, carrying on long conversations with her as if she were still alive. Those who overheard these one-sided discussions were disturbed by their content—Ed would describe his daily activities to his dead mother, ask for her advice on routine decisions, even apologize for things he had done that might have disappointed her.
"I saw Mrs. Peterson in town today, Mother," neighbors heard him say during one of these sessions. "She asked about you, and I told her you were resting. I didn't think you'd want me to discuss family business with outsiders."

The conversations revealed the extent to which Ed's identity had been merged with his mother's. He seemed incapable of making even simple decisions without seeking Augusta's guidance, and when that guidance wasn't forthcoming, he would become paralyzed with anxiety and indecision.

His eating habits became erratic. Augusta had controlled every aspect of his diet, deciding what he would eat and when he would eat it. Without her guidance, Ed seemed unable to plan or prepare meals for himself. Neighbors who brought food found that he would often let it spoil rather than eat it, as if consuming anything without his mother's approval was somehow forbidden.

More disturbing was the way Ed began to modify his behavior to match what he imagined Augusta would want. He started wearing some of her clothing, claiming that it made him feel closer to her. He would eat from her dishes, sleep in her bed when his anxiety became overwhelming, and conduct elaborate rituals designed to maintain some connection with her spirit. "It was like he was trying to become her," Mrs. Hill observed. "He would copy her mannerisms, repeat things she used to say, even walk the way she walked. It was unnatural, the way he was carrying on."

Dr. Kelley, the psychiatrist who would later evaluate Ed after his arrest, would identify this behavior as a severe form of identification with the deceased—a psychological condition in which the survivor attempts to literally merge with the lost person as a way of denying the reality of their death.

"The subject's entire identity had been constructed around his relationship with his mother," Dr. Kelley would write in his report. "When she died, he faced a choice between developing an independent sense of self or attempting to maintain the relationship through identification and fantasy. Unfortunately, he chose the latter option, with consequences that would prove catastrophic."

Spring 1946 - The First Violation

It was sometime in late March or early April 1946 that Ed Gein made his first nocturnal visit to Plainfield Cemetery. He would later claim that he didn't remember making the conscious decision to go there, that he simply found himself walking among the graves in the middle of the night, drawn by forces he couldn't understand or control.

The cemetery was less than two miles from the Gein farmhouse, easily accessible by the network of farm roads that connected the isolated properties in the area. In the months since Augusta's burial, Ed had become obsessed with visiting her grave, initially during daylight hours when such visits might be considered normal expressions of grief.
But his nighttime visits had a different character. Ed would arrive at the cemetery after midnight, when he could be certain of being alone with the dead. He would sit beside Augusta's grave for hours, talking to her, pleading with her to somehow return to him, begging for guidance on how to survive without her presence.

It was during one of these visits that Ed first noticed other graves in the cemetery — particularly those of women who had been recently buried, women who bore some physical resemblance to his mother. The idea that would eventually drive him to commit acts of unthinkable desecration began as a simple curiosity about what death looked like, what happened to bodies after they were placed in the ground.

"I just wanted to see," he would later tell investigators. "I wanted to understand what death was like, what it meant to be buried in the cold ground. I thought maybe if I understood death better, I could understand what had happened to Mother."

The first grave Ed violated belonged to a middle-aged woman named Eleanor Adams, who had died of cancer in February 1946 and been buried in a plot about fifty yards from Augusta's grave. Eleanor had been a quiet, religious woman who bore a passing resemblance to Augusta — the same general build, the same graying hair, the same stern facial features that characterized many farm women of that generation.

Ed's first exhumation was crude and desperate. Using farm tools he had brought from home, he dug down to the casket in the middle of a moonless night, working by feel more than sight to avoid being discovered. When he finally reached Eleanor's body, he found it in the early stages of decomposition but still recognizable as the woman he had occasionally seen in town.

What happened next would set the pattern for all of Ed's subsequent grave robberies. Instead of being revolted by the condition of the corpse, he was fascinated by it. He spent hours examining Eleanor's body, studying the effects of death and burial, touching and manipulating the remains with a clinical detachment that suggested profound psychological disturbance. But Ed didn't simply observe Eleanor's corpse — he began to experiment with it. Using techniques he had learned from butchering animals on the farm, he removed portions of the body, particularly the face and hands, which he wrapped carefully and took back to the farmhouse. His stated goal, he would later claim, was to better understand the process of death and preservation.

"I thought maybe if I could learn how to preserve things, I could keep Mother with me somehow," he explained to investigators. "I thought maybe death wasn't as final as it seemed, maybe there was a way to bring people back or at least keep parts of them alive."

The removed body parts were taken back to the farmhouse, where Ed began his first experiments in what would become an increasingly elaborate and disturbing practice of preserving and modifying human remains. Using techniques adapted from taxidermy and meat processing, he attempted to tan Eleanor's facial skin, to preserve her hands, to create what he would later describe as "keepsakes" that would allow him to maintain some connection with the dead.

These early experiments were largely unsuccessful. Ed lacked the knowledge and equipment necessary for proper preservation, and most of the material he removed from Eleanor's grave quickly decomposed beyond use. But the psychological satisfaction he derived from the process — the sense that he was somehow transcending the finality of death — was enough to ensure that he would repeat the experience. Over the following months, Ed would violate at least six more graves in Plainfield Cemetery, always choosing women who bore some resemblance to his mother, always working under cover of darkness to avoid detection. Each exhumation taught him more about the preservation process, and each successful preservation gave him a greater sense of control over death itself.

1946-1950 - The Years of Experimentation

As Ed's grave robbing activities became more frequent and more sophisticated, he began to develop what could only be described as a workshop for processing human remains in the farmhouse that had once been his childhood home. The basement, which Augusta had rarely visited due to her arthritis, became the center of operations for experiments that grew increasingly elaborate and disturbing with each passing month.

Ed's stated goal during this period was to find ways to preserve and modify human remains that would allow him to maintain some connection with his dead mother. But investigators would later conclude that his activities had evolved far beyond simple preservation into something that resembled a macabre form of art or craft work.

Using tools and techniques adapted from his experience with farm animals, Ed began creating household items from the human remains he collected during his cemetery visits. He fashioned bowls from skulls, made lampshades from facial skin, created chair seats from strips of human hide. Each item was crafted with meticulous attention to detail, as if Ed were trying to create a complete domestic environment populated by reminders of the dead.

The psychological motivation behind these activities became clearer as Ed's behavior during this period was later analyzed by mental health professionals. Dr. Kelley's evaluation would conclude that Ed was attempting to recreate his relationship with his mother through contact with death and the dead.

"The subject's activities represent an attempt to transcend the finality of death through incorporation of human remains into his daily environment," Dr. Kelley wrote. "By surrounding himself with objects created from human bodies, particularly those of women who resembled his mother, he was attempting to maintain the sense of maternal presence that had been the organizing principle of his entire existence."

But Ed's experiments went beyond simple preservation and craft work. He began to study anatomy and physiology, teaching himself through trial and error how human bodies were constructed and how they could be modified. His goal, he would later explain, was to understand the essential differences between male and female anatomy so that he could somehow transform himself into a woman—specifically, into his mother.

"I wanted to become her," he told Dr. Kelley during one of their sessions. "I thought maybe if I could understand how women's bodies were different from men's bodies, I could find a way to change myself, to become the person Mother wanted me to be."

This desire for transformation led Ed to begin working on what he would later describe as his masterpiece—a complete "woman suit" created from the torsos and organs of female corpses. The suit was designed to be worn like clothing, allowing Ed to literally inhabit a female body and experience what he imagined was the essence of womanhood.

The construction of the woman suit required Ed to become increasingly bold in his grave robbing activities. He needed fresher corpses, bodies that had not been buried long enough to decompose significantly. This requirement led him to expand his operations beyond Plainfield Cemetery to other burial grounds in the area, always seeking recently deceased women who met his specific criteria.

But even fresh corpses had limitations. The bodies Ed exhumed were often in states of decomposition that made them difficult to work with, and the preservation techniques he had taught himself were not sophisticated enough to maintain human tissue indefinitely. He began to realize that his experiments would be more successful if he had access to truly fresh material— bodies that had not been subjected to the burial process at all.

This realization would prove to be the crucial step in Ed's evolution from grave robber to murderer.

1950-1954 - The Transition to Murder

The exact moment when Ed Gein decided to commit his first murder remains unknown, but investigators would later conclude that the transition from grave robbing to killing was probably gradual rather than sudden. His increasing frustration with the quality of exhumed bodies, combined with his growing confidence in his ability to avoid detection, created conditions that made murder almost inevitable.

During this period, Ed's behavior became increasingly strange even by his own unusual standards. Neighbors reported seeing lights in the farmhouse at all hours of the night, hearing sounds that suggested heavy work being done in the basement, finding Ed walking along country roads in the middle of the night carrying bundles or packages that he would hide when approached.

His social interactions, which had always been limited, became almost nonexistent. Ed would go weeks without speaking to another living person, spending all his time either working on his preservation projects or conducting elaborate rituals designed to maintain contact with his dead mother. The farmhouse itself began to reflect Ed's deteriorating mental state. Rooms that had once been kept neat and orderly became cluttered with newspapers, magazines, and household items that hadn't been used or cleaned in years. But mixed in with the ordinary debris were objects that revealed the true nature of Ed's activities—skulls used as bowls, furniture upholstered with human skin, lampshades made from preserved faces.

Ed's transformation of the farmhouse into what investigators would later describe as a "house of horrors" was not random or chaotic. Instead, it represented a systematic attempt to create an environment that reflected his psychological state—a place where death and life were blended together, where the boundaries between past and present were erased, where his mother's presence could be felt in every room.

"He was trying to create a world where death didn't exist," Dr. Kelley would later observe. "By surrounding himself with objects made from human remains, by engaging in elaborate rituals designed to communicate with the dead, by transforming his living space into something that resembled a tomb, he was attempting to exist in a reality where his mother was still alive and still in control of his existence."

But this artificial reality was inherently unstable. The preserved human remains that filled the farmhouse gradually decomposed despite Ed's efforts to maintain them. The conversations he held with his dead mother became increasingly one-sided as her imagined presence grew fainter with time. Most importantly, the bodies he exhumed from local cemeteries were often too degraded to serve his purposes effectively.

Ed needed fresher material, and by 1954, he was psychologically prepared to kill to get it.

December 8, 1954 - The First Murder

Mary Hogan was fifty-one years old when she encountered Ed Gein for the last time on a snowy December evening in 1954. A tough, independent woman who had been running her tavern for several years, Mary was known throughout the area as someone who could handle difficult customers and wasn't afraid to speak her mind. She was also known to bear a striking physical resemblance to Augusta Gein—a resemblance that would prove fatal.

Ed had been visiting Mary's tavern sporadically for several months, always arriving alone and usually ordering just a single beer that he would nurse for hours while studying the other customers. Mary had noticed his unusual behavior but hadn't considered him particularly threatening. He was strange, certainly, but he was always polite and never caused trouble. What Mary didn't understand was that Ed had been studying her, memorizing her features, comparing her appearance to his mental image of his mother. In his increasingly distorted perception, Mary Hogan had begun to represent a potential replacement for Augusta — a living woman who could be transformed into the maternal figure he so desperately needed.

The tavern was nearly empty on the evening of December 8, with only a few regular customers nursing drinks and talking quietly among themselves. Mary was working alone, as she often did during the slower weekday periods. When Ed arrived around 8:30 PM, she greeted him with the same professional courtesy she showed all her customers. "Evening, Ed. The usual?"

"Evening, Mrs. Hogan. Yes, just a beer."

What happened next would be reconstructed from physical evidence and Ed's later confessions, since there were no witnesses to the actual killing. According to Ed's account, he had been sitting at the bar for about an hour when Mary made some comment that reminded him of something his mother used to say. The resemblance was so strong that Ed began to believe, in his distorted mental state, that Mary actually was his mother — that Augusta had somehow returned to him in the form of this tavern owner.

"I thought she was Mother," Ed would later tell investigators. "She looked like Mother, she talked like Mother, she moved like Mother. I thought God had sent her back to me, and I needed to take her home where she belonged."

Ed's version of events was almost certainly a rationalization constructed after the fact, but the basic sequence of actions was probably accurate. At some point during the evening, he produced a .32 caliber revolver that he had brought from the farm and shot Mary Hogan once in the head. The shot was fired at close range, killing her instantly.

With Mary dead, Ed faced the practical problem of removing her body from the tavern without being detected. This turned out to be easier than he had anticipated. The tavern's back door opened onto an alley where Ed had parked his pickup truck, and the snowy weather meant that few people were moving around the area. He was able to load Mary's body into the truck and drive back to the farm without encountering anyone who might have questioned his activities.

The tavern was discovered empty the next morning by a customer who found the front door unlocked and Mary nowhere to be found. There were signs of a struggle — overturned chairs, broken glass, blood on the floor — but no clear indication of what had happened to the missing woman. Local law enforcement launched an investigation, but with no witnesses and no obvious suspects, the case quickly went cold. Mary Hogan's disappearance was attributed to any number of possibilities — robbery gone wrong, domestic violence, simple abandonment of a business that may have been failing. No one suspected that the quiet bachelor farmer who occasionally stopped by for a beer had committed murder.

Meanwhile, Ed had taken Mary's body back to the farmhouse, where he could finally work with truly fresh human material. Using the techniques he had developed through years of experimenting with exhumed corpses, he began the process of transforming Mary Hogan into the collection of preserved remains that would eventually be discovered by investigators in 1957.

Mary's murder marked a crucial turning point in Ed's psychological development. He had crossed the line from disturbing the dead to creating the dead, from grave robbing to murder. And the satisfaction he derived from having access to fresh, intact human material would ensure that Mary Hogan would not be his last victim.

The monster that Augusta Gein had created through years of psychological manipulation and control had finally emerged fully formed. The question was no longer whether Ed would kill again, but when and how he would select his next victim.

The answer would come nearly three years later, on a snowy morning in December 1957, when Bernice Worden made the fatal mistake of being alone in her hardware store when Ed Gein decided he needed fresh material for his increasingly elaborate experiments.
To be continued...

Chapter 6:
The Final Hunt

November 14, 1957 - Two Days Before

Bernice Worden was arranging a display of hunting supplies when Ed Gein walked into her hardware store for what would prove to be his reconnaissance visit. The Wisconsin deer hunting season was about to begin, and her store was busier than usual with hunters stocking up on ammunition, licenses, and equipment for the annual ritual that defined autumn in rural Wisconsin.

Ed moved through the store with the casual demeanor of a regular customer, examining merchandise, nodding politely to other patrons, engaging in the kind of small talk that had allowed him to blend into the Plainfield community for over a decade. To observers, he appeared to be nothing more than a slightly eccentric local farmer preparing for hunting season like everyone else. But Ed wasn't really shopping that day. He was planning.

For nearly three years, since Mary Hogan's murder had provided him with the fresh human material he needed for his increasingly elaborate experiments, Ed had managed to satisfy his psychological needs through a combination of grave robbing and the preservation work he conducted in the farmhouse basement. The woman suit he had been constructing was nearly complete, and the collection of household items made from human remains had grown to fill several rooms of the deteriorating house.

But by late 1957, Ed's supply of usable material was running low. The corpses he exhumed from local cemeteries were often too decomposed to serve his purposes, and his preservation techniques, while improved through years of practice, were still not sophisticated enough to maintain human tissue indefinitely. He was beginning to realize that he would need to kill again.

The selection of his next victim was not random. Ed had been observing the women of Plainfield for months, studying their routines, evaluating their suitability for his purposes. He needed someone who worked alone, someone whose disappearance might not be immediately noticed, someone who bore at least a passing resemblance to the maternal figure who continued to dominate his psychological landscape.

Bernice Worden met all of these criteria. She ran her hardware store largely by herself, often working alone for hours at a time. She was a widow with grown children who lived independently, meaning her absence from home might not be discovered immediately. Most importantly, she was a woman in her late fifties with graying hair and stern features that reminded Ed of his mother.

"Need anything special today, Ed?" Bernice asked as he approached the counter with a container of antifreeze—a purchase that would provide him with a plausible reason for being in the store while he finalized his plans.
"Just this, Mrs. Worden. Getting ready for winter."

As Bernice recorded the sale in her ledger, Ed studied the layout of the store with the methodical attention of someone planning a crime. He noted the location of the cash register, observed the sight lines from the street, identified the back door that led to the alley where he could park his truck without being seen by passing traffic.

Most importantly, he confirmed that Bernice would be working alone on Saturday morning. Her son Frank had mentioned during casual conversation that he would be out of town on official business, and Ed had observed that Saturday mornings were typically quiet periods when few customers visited the store.

"I might stop by Saturday for some more supplies," Ed mentioned casually as he prepared to leave. "What time do you usually open?" "Eight o'clock sharp, same as always. I'll be here."

Those words would seal Bernice Worden's fate. As Ed walked out of the store that November afternoon, he was already visualizing how her murder would unfold, how he would transport her body back to the farm, how he would process her remains to create the materials he needed for his ongoing experiments.

For Ed Gein, killing had become a practical necessity rather than an emotional impulse. He needed fresh human material, and murder was the most efficient way to obtain it.

November 15, 1957 - The Day Before

Ed spent Friday in careful preparation for what he had already decided would be Bernice Worden's last day of life. The methodical planning that went into his crimes was one of the aspects that most disturbed investigators when they finally understood the full scope of his activities. This wasn't the impulsive violence of someone who had snapped under pressure — it was the calculated behavior of someone who had come to view murder as a routine solution to a recurring problem.

The .22 caliber rifle he selected for the killing was one that Bernice herself had sold him several months earlier. Ed had purchased it ostensibly for hunting small game around the farm, but he had been planning its use for a very different kind of hunting. The irony that Bernice would be killed with a weapon from her own inventory was not lost on Ed, though it's unclear whether he appreciated the dark humor of the situation or simply saw it as a practical convenience.

Ed's preparation extended beyond simply selecting a weapon. He spent Friday cleaning and organizing the basement workshop where he would process Bernice's body, arranging his tools and materials for maximum efficiency. He had learned from experience that the immediate hours after a killing were crucial—the longer he delayed in beginning the preservation process, the more difficult his work would become.

The psychological state that allowed Ed to plan a murder with such clinical detachment was the result of years of gradual desensitization to violence and death. His progression from grave robbing to murder had been so gradual that he no longer experienced the moral revulsion that would prevent most people from even contemplating such acts. In his distorted worldview, killing Bernice Worden was no different from butchering a farm animal—both were simply necessary steps in the process of obtaining materials he needed.

Dr. Kelley would later observe that Ed's ability to compartmentalize his criminal activities represented a severe form of dissociation that allowed him to function normally in social situations while planning and committing acts of extraordinary violence.

"The subject appears to have developed two distinct personality modes," Dr. Kelley wrote in his evaluation. "In social situations, he could present as a harmless, slightly eccentric local resident. But when engaged in criminal activities, he operated with the methodical efficiency of someone for whom violence had become completely normalized."

This dissociation was evident in Ed's behavior on Friday evening, when he attended a community gathering at the local church—the same church where Bernice Worden was a regular congregant. Witnesses would later recall that Ed seemed perfectly normal that night, engaging in casual conversation with neighbors, even speaking politely with Bernice herself when their paths crossed in the church hall.

"He seemed just like always," Mrs. Peterson would later tell investigators. "Maybe a little quieter than usual, but nothing that would make you think he was planning something terrible. He even held the door for Mrs. Worden when she was leaving. If someone had told me then what he was going to do the next morning, I would have said they were crazy."

But Ed's politeness that evening was not evidence of a last-minute change of heart or moral awakening. Instead, it represented the calculated behavior of someone who understood the importance of maintaining his facade of normalcy right up until the moment he struck. By appearing completely ordinary on Friday night, he reduced the likelihood that anyone would suspect his involvement in whatever happened to Bernice on Saturday morning.

As Ed walked home from the church that evening, he was already visualizing the next day's events in precise detail. He knew exactly what time he would arrive at the hardware store, exactly how he would position himself to avoid being seen from the street, exactly what he would say to Bernice in the moments before he killed her.

The only variable he couldn't control was whether other customers might arrive at an inopportune moment. But Ed had observed the store's patterns long enough to know that Saturday mornings were typically quiet, and he was prepared to wait for the right opportunity if necessary.

What Ed couldn't have anticipated was that his carefully planned crime would be the one that finally exposed his years of hidden activities. The investigation triggered by Bernice Worden's disappearance would uncover not just her murder, but the full scope of the horrors he had been conducting at the isolated farmhouse where he lived alone with his collection of human remains.

November 16, 1957 - 9:30 AM - The Last Customer

The bell above the door of Worden's Hardware Store chimed for the final time in Bernice Worden's life at exactly 9:30 AM on Saturday, November 16, 1957. Ed Gein entered the store carrying the .22 caliber rifle he had purchased from Bernice several months earlier, moving with the calm confidence of someone who had rehearsed every detail of what was about to unfold.

Bernice was behind the counter, updating inventory records in the ledger she kept beside the old brass cash register. She looked up as Ed approached, greeting him with the same professional courtesy she had shown him for years. "Morning, Ed. What can I help you with today?"

"Morning, Mrs. Worden. I was wondering if you had any antifreeze in stock."

It was the same item he had purchased during his reconnaissance visit two days earlier — a detail that would later help investigators understand how carefully Ed had planned the murder. He needed a plausible reason for being in the store, and antifreeze was a common enough purchase during Wisconsin winters that it wouldn't seem suspicious.

As Bernice moved toward the automotive section to retrieve the antifreeze, Ed followed her, positioning himself so that his back was to the front windows. He had calculated the angles carefully during his previous visits, ensuring that anyone passing by on the street would not be able to see what was about to happen behind the counter.

"Here you go," Bernice said, returning with a red container of antifreeze. "That'll be $1.85."

As she opened the sales ledger to record the transaction, Ed raised the rifle and shot her once in the back of the head. The .22 caliber bullet was small but lethal at close range. Bernice died instantly, collapsing behind the counter without making a sound that might have alerted anyone outside the store. Ed had chosen his weapon carefully — the small-caliber rifle was quiet enough that the shot might not be heard over the normal sounds of Saturday morning activity in downtown Plainfield.

With Bernice dead, Ed faced the practical challenge of removing her body from the store without being detected. This was the moment of greatest risk in his plan, the point at which discovery was most likely. But Ed had prepared for this contingency as carefully as he had planned the murder itself. He moved quickly to the back of the store, unlocking the rear door that opened onto the alley where he had parked his pickup truck. The truck was positioned so that its bed was directly adjacent to the door, minimizing the distance he would need to carry Bernice's body. Ed had even brought a tarp to wrap the corpse, reducing the likelihood that blood would be visible to anyone who might see him loading his truck.

The transfer took less than five minutes. Ed wrapped Bernice's body in the tarp, carried it to his truck, and loaded it into the bed along with the brass cash register he had decided to take as well. The register was heavy and awkward, but Ed had realized that its theft would make Bernice's disappearance look like a robbery gone wrong, potentially misdirecting the investigation away from more personal motives.

Before leaving the store, Ed made a hasty attempt to clean up the blood that had pooled behind the counter. He used rags from the store's inventory to wipe up the most obvious stains, but he lacked the time and materials necessary to eliminate all traces of what had occurred. Dark stains remained visible on the wooden floor, and droplets of blood marked the path from the counter to the back door.

These traces would prove crucial when Bernice's son Frank discovered the scene several hours later. The blood evidence, combined with the missing cash register and the unlocked back door, would immediately alert investigators that they were dealing with foul play rather than a simple missing person case.

But as Ed drove his truck down the rural roads that led back to his farm, he was confident that his crime would go undetected long enough for him to complete his work with Bernice's body. He had no way of knowing that Frank Worden's concern for his mother would lead to the discovery of the crime scene that same evening, or that the investigation triggered by Bernice's disappearance would finally expose the horrors he had been hiding for over a decade.

November 16, 1957 - 10:15 AM
The Return to the Farm

The drive from Worden's Hardware Store to the Gein farm took approximately fifteen minutes along country roads that were largely deserted on Saturday morning. Ed encountered only two other vehicles during the journey — a farmer driving a tractor and a delivery truck heading toward town — and neither driver appeared to take any special notice of his pickup truck or its concealed cargo.

Ed's confidence during the drive reflected his years of experience in transporting human remains without detection. Since beginning his grave robbing activities in 1946, he had made dozens of similar trips, carrying exhumed bodies from various cemeteries back to his farmhouse workshop. The main difference this time was that his cargo was fresh rather than decomposed, a factor that would make his subsequent work both easier and more satisfying.

The Gein farmhouse sat at the end of a long dirt driveway, surrounded by fields and outbuildings that provided complete privacy for whatever activities Ed chose to conduct there. No neighbors were close enough to observe his comings and goings, and the isolation that had once protected him from his mother's fears about outside corruption now shielded him from detection as he engaged in acts that defied comprehension.

Ed backed his truck up to the small outbuilding that locals knew as a summer kitchen — the same structure where investigators would later discover Bernice's mutilated corpse. The building had originally been used for canning and food preparation during the warmer months, but Ed had converted it into a supplementary workspace for his human preservation projects.

The process of unloading Bernice's body and positioning it for the work he planned to do was routine by this point in Ed's criminal career. He had developed efficient methods for moving and positioning corpses, techniques refined through years of practice with both exhumed and freshly killed victims. What made this murder significant was not the killing itself, but the fact that it would finally expose Ed's activities to law enforcement.

Ed's first step was to hang Bernice's body from the rafters of the summer kitchen, suspending it by ropes tied around the ankles in the same manner he would use to dress a deer during hunting season. This positioning allowed him to work on the corpse more easily while also ensuring that blood would drain away from the body cavity.

Using butchering techniques he had learned from processing farm animals, Ed then proceeded to decapitate and gut Bernice's corpse with the methodical efficiency of someone who had performed similar operations many times before. The head was removed cleanly and set aside for later processing, while the body cavity was completely cleaned out and prepared for whatever use Ed had planned for it.

The entire process took several hours and required considerable physical effort, but Ed approached the work with the calm concentration of someone engaged in a familiar task. There was nothing frenzied or emotional about his treatment of Bernice's remains — it was simply a job that needed to be done to obtain the materials he required for his ongoing projects.

What Ed couldn't have known was that his carefully planned crime had already begun to unravel. Even as he worked in the summer kitchen, transforming Bernice Worden from a living person into raw material for his experiments, her son Frank was becoming increasingly concerned about her failure to return home for dinner.

By evening, Frank's concern would lead him to the hardware store, where he would discover the blood evidence that would trigger an immediate investigation. Within hours, that investigation would focus on Ed Gein as the primary suspect, and by the following evening, law enforcement officers would be standing outside the very building where Ed was conducting his grisly work.

November 16, 1957 - 8:45 PM - The Discovery

Sheriff Art Schley's patrol car pulled into the yard of the Gein farm just as the last light was fading from the western sky. The property looked exactly as it always had—rundown, cluttered, slightly abandoned—but tonight there was something different about the atmosphere that made both Schley and Deputy Worden approach with unusual caution.

Ed emerged from one of the outbuildings as the patrol car came to a stop, moving with his characteristic shuffling gait but seeming more nervous than usual. In the beam of Schley's flashlight, his clothes appeared to be stained with what might have been blood, though it was difficult to be certain in the poor light.

"Evening, Ed," Sheriff Schley called out. "We need to ask you some questions about Bernice Worden."
The conversation that followed would be analyzed by law enforcement officials and psychologists for years to come. Ed's responses were polite and seemingly cooperative, but there was an underlying tension that suggested he was working hard to maintain his composure. When asked about his whereabouts during the day, he provided an alibi that was detailed enough to sound rehearsed.

"I was visiting Henry Hill most of the afternoon," Ed said, referring to a neighbor who lived several miles away. "You can ask him if you want. We were working on his tractor."

But as the questioning continued, small inconsistencies began to emerge in Ed's story. His timeline didn't quite add up, and his explanations for his activities became increasingly elaborate. Most tellingly, he seemed to be directing the officers' attention away from the summer kitchen, positioning himself between them and the building in a way that suggested he was protecting something inside.

Sheriff Schley had been in law enforcement long enough to recognize when someone was hiding something important. Ed's nervous behavior, combined with the blood evidence found at the hardware store, provided sufficient justification for searching the property. When Schley asked for permission to look around, Ed's response would be remembered by everyone present.

"I guess that would be all right," Ed said. "But you won't find anything here."

The emphasis he placed on the word "here" struck both officers as oddly specific, as if he was making a very particular denial about this location while leaving open the possibility that something might be found elsewhere on the property. Sheriff Schley decided to start with the building that Ed seemed most anxious about. As he approached the summer kitchen, a smell became apparent that made his stomach tighten — something sweet and metallic that experienced law enforcement officers learn to associate with death and violence.

The door to the summer kitchen was secured with a simple latch, but it opened easily when Schley lifted it. He shined his flashlight inside, and what he saw would haunt him for the rest of his life.

Hanging from the rafters by ropes tied around the ankles was the decapitated, gutted corpse of what had obviously been a human being. The body had been dressed like a deer, cleaned and prepared with the same methodical precision that any hunter would use on game. But this wasn't a deer—this was Bernice Worden, the woman who had been missing since that morning.

"Jesus Christ," Deputy Worden whispered behind him, his voice barely audible in the frigid air.

For several seconds, both officers stood frozen in the doorway, trying to process what they were seeing. Neither man had ever encountered anything like this before, and the horror of the discovery was compounded by the realization that they had been talking casually with the person responsible just moments earlier.

Sheriff Schley forced himself to examine the scene more carefully, though every instinct screamed at him to turn away. The corpse had been decapitated with surgical precision, and the entire body cavity had been cleaned out completely. Whoever had done this work knew exactly what they were doing—this wasn't the frenzied mutilation that might be expected from someone who had lost control, but rather the methodical work of someone who had performed similar operations before.

As the full implications of the discovery began to sink in, Sheriff Schley realized that they were dealing with something far more serious than a simple murder. The level of skill and planning evident in what had been done to Bernice's body suggested that this was not Ed Gein's first victim, and the casual way he had been living on a property that contained such horrors indicated that there might be additional evidence of other crimes.

"Ed Gein, you're under arrest for the murder of Bernice Worden," Schley announced as he emerged from the summer kitchen.

Ed's response was not what either officer expected. Instead of denying the charges or expressing surprise at the accusation, he simply nodded, as if acknowledging that his secret had finally been discovered. There was almost a sense of relief in his demeanor, as if maintaining the facade of normalcy had become too exhausting to continue.

As they handcuffed the soft-spoken farmer who had shocked them with the horror concealed in his outbuilding, neither Sheriff Schley nor Deputy Worden could have imagined what they would discover when they finally gained access to the main farmhouse. The summer kitchen had contained only the most recent evidence of Ed Gein's activities—the full scope of his crimes was waiting to be uncovered in the deteriorating house where he had lived alone since his mother's death twelve years earlier.

The quiet bachelor farmer who helped neighbors with their chores and tipped his hat to ladies on the street had been revealed as something far more disturbing than anyone in Plainfield could have imagined. But the discovery of Bernice Worden's mutilated corpse was only the beginning of a nightmare that would shake not just the residents of this small farming community, but the entire nation.

Within hours, investigators would uncover evidence of crimes that defied comprehension, horrors that would inspire decades of books and movies, and a level of psychological disturbance that would forever change how America understood the monsters that could be hiding behind facades of rural politeness and community respectability.

The arrest of Ed Gein marked the end of more than a decade of hidden crimes, but it was also the beginning of a much larger investigation that would reveal the true extent of what could happen when psychological damage was allowed to fester in complete isolation from normal human contact and moral guidance.
To be continued...

Chapter 7:

Inside the Nightmare

November 17, 1957 - 6:00 AM -
The Morning After

The news of Ed Gein's arrest spread through Plainfield like wildfire, but what investigators discovered inside his farmhouse would prove to be far more shocking than anyone could have imagined. As dawn broke over the isolated property, a team of law enforcement officers, medical personnel, and crime scene specialists prepared to enter what would later be described as one of the most disturbing crime scenes in American history.

Sheriff Art Schley had barely slept after the previous night's arrest. The image of Bernice Worden's mutilated corpse hanging in the summer kitchen haunted him, but he suspected that what they had discovered was only the beginning. Ed's calm acceptance of his arrest, combined with the methodical skill evident in his treatment of the victim, suggested someone who had been engaging in such activities for an extended period.

"We're going to find more," Schley told the assembled team as they gathered outside the farmhouse. "I don't know what we're going to find, but I know there's more. Nobody gets that good at something without practice."

The farmhouse itself looked deceptively normal in the early morning light. It was rundown and cluttered, certainly, but it appeared to be nothing more than the home of an eccentric bachelor farmer. There was no external indication of the horrors that waited inside, no sign that the building contained evidence of crimes that would shock the nation.

Dr. George Morrison, the county coroner who had been called to assist with the investigation, approached the front door with the clinical detachment of someone who had spent decades dealing with death in its many forms. But even his extensive experience had not prepared him for what lay beyond the threshold of Ed Gein's home.

The smell hit them first—a mixture of decay, unwashed clothing, and something else that several investigators would later describe as the distinctive odor of death. But it wasn't the overwhelming stench that might be expected from a house containing multiple corpses. Instead, it was more subtle, as if the scent of mortality had permeated the very walls of the building over many years.

As they stepped inside, the investigators found themselves in a world that seemed to exist outside the normal boundaries of human experience. Every room was cluttered with accumulated debris—newspapers, magazines, broken furniture, farm tools, and household items that appeared to have been abandoned exactly where they were last used. But mixed in with the ordinary detritus of daily life were objects that defied comprehension.

Deputy Martinez was the first to spot the skull sitting on a cluttered table in what had once been the kitchen. At first glance, it looked like it might be some kind of unusual bowl or decorative item. But closer examination revealed that it was a human skull that had been carefully modified, with the top portion sawed off and the interior cleaned and polished to create a functional container.

"Sheriff, you need to see this," Martinez called out, his voice carefully controlled despite the obvious shock of his discovery.

As the investigation team spread out through the house, more disturbing items came to light with each passing minute. In the living room, they found four chairs whose seats had been replaced with strips of human skin that had been carefully tanned and stretched over the wooden frames. The workmanship was meticulous, showing a level of skill that suggested extensive practice with such materials.

On a table near the chairs sat a lampshade that, upon closer inspection, proved to be made from a human face. The facial features were still clearly visible—lips, nose, eyelashes—and the skin had been preserved with such skill that it retained a lifelike appearance. An electrical cord ran through the mouth, allowing the grotesque creation to function as an actual lamp. Dr. Morrison, who had been documenting each discovery with clinical precision, found himself struggling to maintain his professional composure as the full scope of what they were dealing with became apparent. "This isn't the work of someone who simply snapped," he told Sheriff Schley. "This level of preservation, this attention to detail—whoever did this has been practicing for years."

As they moved deeper into the house, the discoveries became even more disturbing. In what appeared to be a bedroom, investigators found ten human skulls hanging on the walls like hunting trophies. Some still had hair attached, others had been completely cleaned and polished. Several showed evidence of modification—holes drilled for hanging, or tops sawed off to create the skull bowls they had found elsewhere in the house.

But perhaps most chilling was the discovery made in a paper bag sitting on a cluttered dresser: the preserved heads of two women, wrapped in brown paper like groceries from the local market. The heads were in excellent condition, suggesting they had been removed from recently deceased victims and preserved using techniques that Ed had refined over years of practice.

November 17, 1957 - 10:30 AM
The Workshop

The basement of the Gein farmhouse revealed the true scope of Ed's activities. What investigators found there was nothing less than a fully equipped workshop for processing human remains, complete with specialized tools, preservation chemicals, and work surfaces that showed evidence of extensive use.

The basement had been divided into several distinct areas, each apparently dedicated to a different aspect of Ed's macabre hobby. One corner contained what appeared to be a dissection area, with a large table surrounded by various knives, saws, and other cutting implements. Dark stains on the table and floor suggested that this area had seen considerable use over the years.

Another section had been set up for what could only be described as a tanning operation. Wooden frames held strips of human skin in various stages of the preservation process, while containers of chemicals used for treating hides sat nearby. The level of organization and the variety of equipment suggested someone who had been engaged in such activities for years and had refined his techniques through extensive practice.

Dr. Morrison's examination of the preservation equipment revealed a level of sophistication that was both impressive and deeply disturbing. "He's been teaching himself anatomy and preservation techniques," Morrison told the other investigators. "Some of this work shows real skill. He understands how to properly process and preserve human tissue."

The most disturbing discovery in the basement was what Ed would later describe as his "masterpiece" — a complete vest made from the torso of a female victim, including breasts and female genitalia. The garment had been carefully crafted with string ties that would allow someone to wear it like clothing. The psychological implications of such an item were staggering, suggesting someone who was attempting to literally transform himself into a woman through the use of human remains. Additional items found in the basement included belts made from human skin, complete with nipples still attached; a collection of human noses stored in a shoebox; and various organs that had been preserved and stored for unknown purposes. Each item showed the same meticulous attention to detail, the same careful workmanship that characterized all of Ed's creations.

But what truly shocked the investigators was the sheer volume of human remains they were discovering. Based on the number of skulls, the variety of preserved body parts, and the extensive nature of Ed's collection, it was clear that he had been obtaining human material from multiple sources over an extended period of time.

"How many people are we talking about here?" Deputy Worden asked as they catalogued item after item made from human remains.

Dr. Morrison's answer would prove to be prophetic: "More than we'll probably ever know for certain."

November 17, 1957 - 2:00 PM

The Confessions Begin

While investigators continued their work at the farmhouse, Ed Gein sat in a jail cell in Wautoma, the county seat, apparently eager to discuss his activities with anyone willing to listen. His confessions, which would continue for days, revealed a mind that had completely normalized acts that most people would find unthinkable.

When questioned about the items found in his house, Ed showed no apparent understanding of why others found them disturbing. He spoke about his preservation work with the same casual tone that another person might use to discuss a hobby like woodworking or gardening. There was no evidence of guilt, remorse, or even awareness that his activities were considered wrong by normal standards.
"I needed those things," Ed explained when asked about the household items made from human remains. "The house felt empty after Mother died. I was just trying to make it feel more like home."

His explanation for the woman suit was even more disturbing: "I wanted to see what it would be like to be a woman. I thought if I could wear something like that, I could understand how Mother felt, what it was like to be her."
Ed's confessions also revealed the extent of his grave robbing activities. He admitted to violating at least nine graves in local cemeteries, always choosing recently buried women who bore some resemblance to his mother. He described these activities in the same matter-of-fact tone he used to discuss his murders, showing no awareness that desecrating graves was considered a serious crime.

"I was curious about death," he explained. "I wanted to understand what happened to people after they died, what they looked like under the ground. I thought maybe if I understood death better, I could find a way to bring Mother back." When questioned about the murders of Mary Hogan and Bernice Worden, Ed's responses were equally chilling. He spoke about killing these women as if it were a practical necessity, a solution to the problem of obtaining fresh material for his experiments.

"The bodies from the cemetery weren't very good anymore," he explained. "They were too old, too decayed. I needed fresher material if I wanted to do good work."

Dr. Edward Kelley, the psychiatrist brought in to evaluate Ed's mental state, was struck by the complete absence of normal emotional responses to his crimes. "The subject shows no evidence of guilt, remorse, or even understanding that his actions were wrong," Dr. Kelley noted in his initial evaluation. "He speaks about murder and mutilation with the same emotional tone that most people would use to discuss routine household chores."

November 18, 1957 - The Media Circus

By the second day of the investigation, news of the discoveries at the Gein farm had spread far beyond Plainfield. Reporters from newspapers and radio stations across the Midwest descended on the small farming community, transforming it into a media circus that overwhelmed local law enforcement's ability to maintain order.

The story that emerged from initial news reports was so bizarre that many readers initially assumed it was some kind of hoax or exaggeration. Tales of furniture made from human skin, lampshades crafted from faces, and a "woman suit" constructed from female torsos seemed too grotesque to be real. But as more details emerged and official sources confirmed the discoveries, the American public was forced to confront the reality that such horrors could exist in their midst.

The national media attention had profound effects on the residents of Plainfield, who found themselves at the center of a story that portrayed their community as the home of a monster. Many residents expressed shock and disbelief that someone they had known for years could have been capable of such acts. "He seemed so normal," was a refrain heard repeatedly from neighbors and townspeople. "He was quiet, maybe a little strange, but he was always polite. He helped people with their farm work, he went to church. How could someone like that do such terrible things?"

The question of how Ed Gein had managed to hide his activities for so many years while maintaining a facade of normalcy would become one of the most disturbing aspects of the case. It suggested that the most dangerous predators might be those who appeared most harmless, most integrated into their communities.

Local business owners found themselves dealing with an influx of curiosity seekers who had driven to Plainfield hoping to get a glimpse of the farm where such horrors had taken place. Some entrepreneurs attempted to capitalize on the notoriety by selling "souvenirs" and offering tours of sites connected to the case. But most residents were simply horrified by the attention and eager for the media circus to end.

The investigation itself was complicated by the level of public interest and the pressure from media outlets for constant updates. Sheriff Schley found himself conducting multiple press conferences per day, trying to satisfy the public's appetite for information while also protecting the integrity of an ongoing investigation.

"We're dealing with crimes that go back years, possibly decades," Schley told reporters. "It's going to take time to properly investigate all the evidence we've found and to determine the full scope of what we're dealing with."

November 19, 1957

The Psychological Profile

As Dr. Kelley continued his evaluation of Ed Gein, a clearer picture began to emerge of the psychological factors that had contributed to his transformation from an eccentric loner into a killer who collected human remains. The psychiatrist's findings would prove crucial in understanding not just Ed's individual pathology, but the broader question of how such extreme criminal behavior could develop without detection. Dr. Kelley's initial assessment focused on Ed's relationship with his mother and the psychological damage caused by years of extreme overprotection and isolation. "The subject's entire identity was constructed around his relationship with his deceased mother," Dr. Kelley noted. "When she died, he faced a psychological crisis that he attempted to resolve through contact with death and the dead."

The psychiatrist identified several key factors that had contributed to Ed's criminal development:

Extreme Social Isolation: Ed's lack of normal social relationships had prevented him from developing the kinds of emotional connections that might have provided alternatives to his obsession with his mother. Without friends, romantic relationships, or even casual social interactions, he had no external reference points for normal behavior.

Arrested Psychological Development: Years of overprotection had prevented Ed from developing the independence and decision-making skills that characterize normal adult functioning. At age fifty-one, he had the emotional maturity of a much younger person, making him unable to cope with loss or change in healthy ways.

Identification with the Deceased: Rather than accepting his mother's death and gradually adapting to life without her, Ed had attempted to maintain their relationship through elaborate fantasies and rituals. His collection of human remains represented an attempt to literally surround himself with death as a way of staying connected to his deceased mother.

Complete Absence of Moral Development: Ed showed no evidence of having developed a normal moral compass or understanding of right and wrong. His actions were guided entirely by his psychological needs rather than by any consideration of their effects on others or their violation of social norms.

Dr. Kelley's evaluation also revealed the extent to which Ed's crimes were driven by a desire for transformation rather than simple violence. "The subject's ultimate goal appears to have been to literally become his mother through the incorporation of female characteristics obtained from his victims," the psychiatrist wrote. "This represents a severe form of gender dysphoria complicated by necrophilia and an inability to distinguish between fantasy and reality."

The psychological profile that emerged from Dr. Kelley's work would have profound implications for the legal proceedings that would follow. It raised serious questions about Ed's competency to stand trial and his ability to understand the nature of his crimes.

November 20, 1957

The Community Reckons

As the initial shock of the discoveries began to wear off, the residents of Plainfield were forced to confront some uncomfortable questions about their community and their own failure to recognize the signs of Ed's criminal activities. The investigation had revealed that Ed's transformation from grave robber to murderer had taken place over more than a decade, during which time he had continued to interact with neighbors and community members on a regular basis.

How had no one noticed the smell of decay coming from his property? How had no one questioned the strange sounds and lights that emanated from his farmhouse at all hours of the night? How had no one connected Ed's odd behavior to the disappearances of Mary Hogan and other women who had gone missing over the years?

These questions forced residents to acknowledge that they had collectively chosen to ignore warning signs that, in retrospect, seemed obvious. Ed's strange behavior, his social isolation, his apparent inability to function normally — all of these had been dismissed as harmless eccentricity rather than potential indicators of serious psychological disturbance. "We all knew Eddie was different," admitted Mrs. Hill, one of Ed's closest neighbors. "But different isn't the same as dangerous. He was always polite, always helpful when you needed a hand with something. How were we supposed to know what he was really doing out there?"

The question of community responsibility would continue to haunt Plainfield for years to come. Some residents blamed themselves for not being more observant, for not asking harder questions about Ed's unusual lifestyle. Others argued that there was no way anyone could have predicted the extent of his criminal activities based on his public behavior.

Local religious leaders struggled to provide comfort and explanation for events that seemed to challenge fundamental assumptions about human nature and divine justice. How could God have allowed such evil to exist undetected for so long? What did it say about their community that they had harbored such a monster without knowing it?

Father Murphy, the parish priest at the local Catholic church, spoke for many when he said: "We want to believe that evil announces itself, that monsters look like monsters. But the truth is that evil often hides behind the most ordinary facades. Eddie Gein looked like a harmless farmer, and that's exactly what made him so dangerous."

The discovery of Ed's crimes also had practical effects on the community. Property values in the area plummeted as people became reluctant to live near the site of such horrors. Local businesses suffered as tourism shifted from normal agricultural commerce to morbid curiosity about the "Gein farm." Some residents moved away entirely, unable to continue living in a place that had become synonymous with unspeakable evil.

But perhaps most disturbing was the realization that Ed Gein's case was not unique. As news of the discoveries spread, law enforcement agencies across the country began to re-examine unsolved cases involving missing persons and disturbed individuals who lived in isolation. The Gein case had revealed that the most dangerous criminals might be those who appeared most harmless, most integrated into their communities.

This realization would have lasting effects on American society, contributing to a growing awareness that evil could exist anywhere, hidden behind facades of normalcy and respectability. The age of innocence, when small communities could assume that they knew all their neighbors and that real evil was something that happened in distant cities, had come to an end.

November 21, 1957

The Investigation Continues

As the investigation entered its second week, law enforcement officials were still discovering new evidence at the Gein farm and attempting to identify the various human remains that had been found throughout the property. The task was complicated by the fact that Ed had been collecting and modifying human body parts for more than a decade, making it difficult to determine how many victims were represented in his collection.

Dr. Morrison's examination of the remains had identified parts from at least ten different individuals, but the true number was likely higher. Many of the bones and tissue fragments were too small or too degraded to allow for individual identification, and Ed's practice of combining parts from different victims to create his household items made the forensic analysis extremely challenging.

The investigation had also expanded to include a systematic examination of local cemeteries to determine which graves Ed had violated during his years of nocturnal activities. Cemetery records were cross-referenced with Ed's confessions to identify specific burial sites that had been disturbed, and several graves were exhumed to confirm that bodies had been removed.

This aspect of the investigation proved to be particularly traumatic for the families of the deceased, who were forced to confront the reality that their loved ones' remains had been stolen and desecrated. Many families chose to have their relatives' remains cremated after the investigation was complete, unwilling to risk further violation of their graves.

The scope of the investigation also raised questions about potential accomplices or other individuals who might have been aware of Ed's activities. Despite extensive questioning of neighbors and associates, investigators found no evidence that anyone else had been involved in or aware of his crimes. "He operated completely alone," Sheriff Schley concluded. "Nobody helped him, nobody knew what he was doing, nobody suspected anything. That's what makes this case so frightening — one person was able to carry out these acts for over a decade without anyone catching on."

The investigation's findings would ultimately result in charges related to two murders — those of Mary Hogan and Bernice Worden — as well as multiple counts of grave robbing and desecration of corpses. But the true scope of Ed's crimes would never be fully known, as many of his victims had never been reported missing and many of his activities had left no recoverable evidence.

As the investigation wound down and attention turned to the legal proceedings that would follow, one thing had become clear: Ed Gein's case represented something unprecedented in American criminal history. The combination of murder, grave robbing, and the creation of household items from human remains had created a new category of criminal behavior that challenged existing legal and psychiatric frameworks.

The monster that Augusta Gein had created through years of psychological manipulation and control had finally been captured, but the effects of his crimes would ripple through American society for decades to come. The quiet farming community of Plainfield, Wisconsin, had become forever associated with horrors that defied comprehension, and the name Ed Gein would become synonymous with evil in its most incomprehensible form.

To be continued...

Chapter 8:
The Trial of a Monster

January 16, 1958
Wautoma County Courthouse

The preliminary hearing that would determine Ed Gein's fitness to stand trial took place on a bitter cold morning in January 1958, nearly two months after his arrest. The small courthouse in Wautoma was packed beyond capacity with reporters, curiosity seekers, and local residents who had come to get their first glimpse of the man who had shocked the world with his unspeakable crimes.

Ed sat quietly at the defendant's table, flanked by his court-appointed attorney and appearing remarkably calm for someone facing charges of first-degree murder. At fifty-one years old, he looked like exactly what he had always appeared to be—a harmless, slightly eccentric farmer who wouldn't hurt a fly. The disconnect between his mild appearance and the horrific nature of his crimes would prove to be one of the most disturbing aspects of the entire case.

Judge Robert Gollmar, who had been assigned to oversee the proceedings, was acutely aware that this case would set important precedents for how the legal system dealt with defendants whose crimes defied conventional understanding. The question before the court was not whether Ed Gein had committed the acts he was accused of—his confessions and the physical evidence made his guilt undeniable—but whether he was mentally competent to understand the charges against him and assist in his own defense.

Dr. Edward Kelley took the witness stand to present his psychiatric evaluation, which had been conducted over several weeks of intensive interviews with the defendant. His testimony would prove to be the most crucial element in determining Ed's legal fate.

"In my professional opinion," Dr. Kelley told the packed courtroom, "the defendant suffers from severe mental illness that renders him incapable of understanding the nature of the charges against him or the consequences of his actions. He shows no awareness that his behavior was wrong, no understanding of why others find his actions disturbing, and no ability to distinguish between reality and fantasy when it comes to his relationship with the deceased."

Dr. Kelley's evaluation had revealed a mind so profoundly damaged that it challenged basic assumptions about criminal responsibility and moral accountability. Ed's crimes were not the result of a temporary breakdown or emotional disturbance, but rather the inevitable product of a psychological development that had been arrested and distorted by decades of extreme maternal control and social isolation.

"The defendant has never developed a normal moral compass," Dr. Kelley continued. "His actions were guided entirely by psychological needs rather than by any consideration of their effects on others. He literally cannot understand why society considers his behavior wrong, because he never learned to think in terms of right and wrong as most people understand those concepts."

The psychiatrist's testimony painted a picture of someone who was fundamentally different from normal human beings, someone whose psychological development had been so severely stunted that he could not be held responsible for his actions in the same way that a mentally competent person would be.

"When I asked the defendant about his victims," Dr. Kelley testified, "he spoke about them with the same emotional tone that most people would use to discuss livestock or raw materials for a craft project. He showed no understanding that these were human beings with families, hopes, fears, and feelings. To him, they were simply sources of material for his preservation work."

January 16, 1958 - The Defence Strategy

Ed's court-appointed attorney, William Belter, faced an almost impossible task in defending a client whose crimes had horrified the nation and whose confessions made denial impossible. The only viable strategy was to argue that Ed was not legally responsible for his actions due to mental illness—a defense that would prove both controversial and unprecedented in Wisconsin legal history.

Belter's argument rested on the premise that Ed's extreme psychological damage made him incapable of forming the criminal intent necessary for a murder conviction. Under Wisconsin law, a defendant could not be held criminally responsible for actions committed while mentally incompetent, but proving such incompetence in a case involving such carefully planned and methodically executed crimes would be extremely difficult.

"Ladies and gentlemen of the court," Belter addressed the packed courtroom, "we are not here to excuse or minimize the terrible things that happened to Mary Hogan and Bernice Worden. We are not here to argue that my client is innocent of causing their deaths. We are here to determine whether a man who has been so severely damaged by a lifetime of psychological abuse can be held responsible for actions that were the inevitable result of that damage."

Belter's strategy involved presenting Ed not as a calculating killer who deserved punishment, but as a victim of circumstances beyond his control—a man whose psychological development had been so severely stunted that he never learned to distinguish between right and wrong, fantasy and reality, appropriate and inappropriate behavior.

"Edward Gein is not evil in any conventional sense," Belter argued. "He is damaged. He is the product of a family situation so abnormal, so psychologically destructive, that it prevented him from developing into a functional human being. Punishing him for the inevitable consequences of that damage would be like punishing a child for actions they don't understand."

The defense presented extensive testimony about Ed's upbringing, focusing on Augusta Gein's extreme control and the psychological isolation that had prevented Ed from developing normal social skills or moral understanding. Neighbors testified about the strange dynamics within the Gein household, the way Augusta had dominated her sons' lives, and the obvious psychological damage that had resulted from such extreme overprotection.

Dr. Kelley's evaluation was central to the defense strategy. His testimony established that Ed's crimes were not the result of evil intent or criminal planning, but rather the inevitable product of a mind that had never learned to function normally. Ed's inability to understand why his actions were wrong, his complete lack of empathy for his victims, and his childlike confusion about social norms all supported the argument that he was not legally responsible for his crimes.

"The defendant's mental age is approximately that of a ten-year-old child," Dr. Kelley testified. "He has never developed the cognitive abilities necessary to understand complex moral concepts or to anticipate the consequences of his actions. Holding him criminally responsible would be like prosecuting a severely mentally disabled person for actions they cannot understand."

January 17, 1958 - The Prosecution's Case

District Attorney Earl Kileen faced the challenge of prosecuting a defendant who had confessed to his crimes but whose mental state made traditional legal proceedings extremely problematic. Kileen's goal was not necessarily to secure a conviction and death sentence, but rather to ensure that Ed was permanently removed from society and placed in an institution where he could never harm anyone again.

"The question before this court is not whether Edward Gein is mentally ill," Kileen told the judge. "That much is obvious to anyone who has seen the evidence of his crimes. The question is whether his mental illness absolves him of responsibility for deliberately and methodically murdering two innocent women."

Kileen's argument focused on the premeditated nature of Ed's crimes, particularly the murder of Bernice Worden. The prosecution presented evidence showing that Ed had planned the killing carefully, had conducted reconnaissance visits to the hardware store, had selected his weapon in advance, and had prepared his farmhouse for processing the victim's body.

"This was not the impulsive act of someone who had lost touch with reality," Kileen argued. "This was a carefully planned and executed murder carried out by someone who understood exactly what he was doing and took steps to avoid detection. The defendant may be mentally ill, but he is not so impaired that he cannot distinguish between right and wrong or understand the consequences of his actions."

The prosecution also emphasized the deliberate nature of Ed's grave robbing activities, pointing out that he had avoided detection for over a decade while violating numerous graves and collecting human remains. Such sustained criminal activity required planning, intelligence, and an understanding of the need to avoid law enforcement—all of which suggested someone who could understand the illegal nature of his actions.

"The defendant knew his activities were wrong," Kileen argued. "That's why he conducted them in secret, why he went to such great lengths to avoid detection, why he lied to investigators when they first questioned him. A person who truly cannot distinguish between right and wrong would not take such elaborate precautions to hide their behavior." Kileen also presented testimony from law enforcement officers who had observed Ed's behavior during his arrest and initial interrogation. Despite his confessions, Ed had shown clear awareness that his activities were considered criminal by others, and he had demonstrated the ability to understand legal concepts and procedures.

"The defendant may have unusual motivations for his crimes," Kileen concluded, "but he is not so mentally impaired that he cannot be held responsible for them. Mental illness is not an automatic excuse for murder, and the deliberate, planned nature of these crimes shows that the defendant retained enough cognitive ability to be held accountable for his actions."

January 18, 1958 - Ed's Own Words

Perhaps the most disturbing aspect of the competency hearing was Ed Gein's own testimony, which revealed a mind so fundamentally different from normal human psychology that many observers struggled to understand how such a person could exist. When called to testify on his own behalf, Ed spoke with the same calm, matter-of-fact tone that had characterized his confessions, showing no apparent understanding of why his actions had caused such horror and revulsion.

"I never meant to hurt anybody," Ed told the court, his voice barely audible in the packed courtroom. "I was just trying to understand things, trying to learn about death and what happens to people when they die. I thought maybe if I could understand those things, I could find a way to bring Mother back."

Ed's testimony revealed the extent to which his crimes had been motivated by his obsession with his deceased mother and his inability to accept the finality of her death. He spoke about Augusta as if she were still alive, still providing guidance and approval for his actions. The psychological merger between mother and son had been so complete that Ed seemed incapable of existing as a separate person.

"Mother was everything to me," Ed continued. "When she died, I didn't know how to live without her. I thought maybe if I could surround myself with things that reminded me of her, if I could learn to be more like her, maybe I could keep her with me somehow."

When questioned about his victims, Ed showed the same disturbing lack of empathy that had characterized his confessions. He spoke about Mary Hogan and Bernice Worden not as human beings who had been murdered, but as sources of material for his preservation work. There was no indication that he understood the suffering he had caused or the impact of his crimes on the victims' families.

"I needed fresh material for my work," Ed explained when asked why he had turned from grave robbing to murder. "The bodies from the cemetery weren't very good anymore. They were too old, too decayed. Mrs. Hogan and Mrs. Worden were just... better quality."

The clinical detachment with which Ed discussed his crimes was perhaps more disturbing than the crimes themselves. He showed no awareness that his victims had been living people with their own hopes, fears, and relationships. To him, they were simply raw materials to be processed and transformed into objects that served his psychological needs. Dr. Kelley, who had spent weeks evaluating Ed, later described his testimony as one of the most chilling examples of complete moral blindness he had ever encountered. "The defendant literally cannot understand why others find his actions disturbing," Dr. Kelley noted. "He speaks about murder and mutilation with the same emotional tone that most people would use to discuss routine household tasks."

Ed's testimony also revealed the extent to which he had been living in a fantasy world where normal rules of behavior didn't apply. He spoke about conversations with his dead mother, about his belief that she continued to guide his actions from beyond the grave, and about his conviction that his preservation work was somehow keeping her alive. "Sometimes I can still hear her talking to me," Ed told the court. "She tells me what I should do, how I should live. She's not really gone—she's just in a different place now, and I'm trying to find a way to join her there."

January 19, 1958 - The Expert Testimony

The competency hearing included testimony from multiple psychiatric experts, each offering their professional opinion on Ed's mental state and his fitness to stand trial. The unanimous conclusion was that Ed suffered from severe mental illness that rendered him incapable of understanding the charges against him or assisting in his own defense.

Dr. Milton Miller, a forensic psychiatrist from Madison, testified that Ed's psychological profile was unlike anything he had encountered in decades of practice. "The defendant exhibits symptoms of multiple psychiatric conditions — severe dissociative disorder, schizophrenia, necrophilia, and what could be termed pathological mother fixation," Dr. Miller told the court. "The combination of these conditions has created a psychological state that is essentially incompatible with normal human functioning."

Dr. Miller's evaluation had focused on Ed's ability to understand legal concepts and participate meaningfully in his own defense. His conclusion was that Ed's mental illness made such participation impossible, not because he lacked intelligence, but because his entire worldview was so distorted that he could not comprehend the legal and moral framework within which his trial would take place.

"The defendant is living in a reality that exists only in his own mind," Dr. Miller explained. "He cannot understand why society considers his actions wrong because he has never learned to think in terms of conventional morality. Expecting him to participate in legal proceedings that are based on concepts he cannot comprehend would be fundamentally unfair."

A third expert, Dr. James Lawson from the University of Wisconsin, provided additional insight into the long-term prognosis for someone with Ed's psychological profile. His evaluation suggested that Ed's mental condition was likely permanent and untreatable given the current state of psychiatric medicine.

"The defendant's psychological development was arrested at a very early age and then severely distorted by years of extreme maternal control," Dr. Lawson testified. "The damage that was done is so fundamental, so deeply ingrained, that it would be virtually impossible to reverse even with intensive treatment. This is not a condition that will improve with time or therapy."

Dr. Lawson's testimony raised disturbing questions about what should be done with someone who was clearly dangerous but not legally responsible for their actions. Traditional criminal justice approaches were inadequate for dealing with someone who could not understand why their behavior was wrong and who would likely continue to pose a threat to society if released.

"The defendant will never be safe to live in normal society," Dr. Lawson concluded. "His psychological needs can only be satisfied through contact with death and human remains. Without intensive supervision, he would almost certainly kill again, not out of malice or evil intent, but because his damaged psyche requires such stimulation to function."

January 20, 1958 - The Ruling

Judge Gollmar's decision on Ed Gein's competency to stand trial would set an important precedent for how the legal system dealt with defendants whose crimes stemmed from severe mental illness. After reviewing all the expert testimony and observing Ed's behavior throughout the proceedings, Judge Gollmar concluded that the defendant was not competent to stand trial due to mental disease or defect.

"This court finds that the defendant, Edward Theodore Gein, suffers from severe mental illness that renders him incapable of understanding the nature of the charges against him or of assisting in his own defense," Judge Gollmar announced to the packed courtroom. "Therefore, the defendant is hereby committed to Central State Hospital for the Criminally Insane for treatment until such time as he may be deemed competent to stand trial."

The ruling meant that Ed would be institutionalized indefinitely, potentially for the rest of his life, without ever being formally convicted of murder. Some observers criticized this outcome, arguing that someone who had committed such heinous crimes should face the full penalty of the law regardless of their mental state. Others praised the decision as a humane recognition that punishment was meaningless when applied to someone who could not understand why they were being punished.

The families of Ed's victims had mixed reactions to the ruling. Some were disappointed that he would not face execution for his crimes, feeling that justice had not been served. Others were relieved that he would be permanently removed from society and could never hurt anyone else.

Frank Worden, Bernice's son, spoke for many when he said: "I don't care if they call him crazy or evil or anything else. All I care about is that he can never do to another family what he did to mine. As long as he's locked up where he can't hurt anyone, that's good enough for me."

The ruling also raised broader questions about the relationship between mental illness and criminal responsibility. Ed Gein's case highlighted the inadequacy of existing legal frameworks for dealing with defendants whose crimes stemmed from severe psychological damage rather than criminal intent.

Legal scholars would debate the implications of the Gein case for decades to come. Some argued that the ruling set a dangerous precedent that could allow other killers to escape punishment by claiming mental illness. Others contended that the case demonstrated the need for more sophisticated approaches to criminal justice that took into account the complex relationship between mental health and criminal behavior.

February 1958 - Life at Central State Hospital

Ed's transfer to Central State Hospital for the Criminally Insane marked the beginning of what would become a twenty-seven-year period of institutionalization. The hospital, located in Waupun, Wisconsin, was specifically designed to house individuals who had committed serious crimes but were deemed mentally incompetent to stand trial.

Dr. E.F. Schubert, the hospital's chief psychiatrist, was responsible for Ed's treatment and for conducting periodic evaluations to determine if he might ever become competent to stand trial. Dr. Schubert's initial assessment confirmed the conclusions reached during the competency hearing — Ed suffered from severe, likely permanent mental illness that made normal legal proceedings impossible.

"The patient shows no understanding of the moral and legal concepts that form the basis of our criminal justice system," Dr. Schubert noted in Ed's admission evaluation. "He speaks about his crimes with complete detachment, as if describing someone else's actions. There is no evidence of guilt, remorse, or even basic understanding that he has done anything wrong."

Ed's behavior at the hospital was generally compliant and non-threatening. He followed institutional routines without complaint, participated in prescribed activities, and caused no disciplinary problems. But his conversations with staff and other patients revealed the persistence of the psychological disturbances that had led to his crimes.

He continued to speak about his mother as if she were still alive, often asking staff if they had seen her or if she had left any messages for him. He would spend hours discussing his preservation work, explaining his techniques with the same enthusiasm that another patient might show when talking about a beloved hobby. Most disturbing, he showed continued interest in death and human anatomy, asking detailed questions about what happened to patients who died at the hospital. Hospital staff were instructed to monitor Ed carefully for any signs that he might attempt to harm himself or others. While he showed no aggressive tendencies, his psychological profile suggested that he might become dangerous if given access to human remains or if placed in situations that triggered his obsessive behaviors.

"The patient requires constant supervision," Dr. Schubert wrote in his quarterly evaluation. "While he presents no immediate physical threat, his psychological needs can only be satisfied through activities that pose extreme danger to others. He must never be allowed unsupervised access to deceased individuals or to tools that could be used for dissection or preservation work."

1968 - The First Competency Review

Ten years after his initial commitment, Ed underwent his first comprehensive competency review to determine if his mental condition had improved enough to allow him to stand trial. The review process involved extensive interviews with hospital staff, psychological testing, and evaluation by independent psychiatric experts.

The results were disappointing for those who hoped that a decade of institutional treatment might have improved Ed's condition. If anything, his psychological state had deteriorated further during his years at Central State Hospital. The isolation from normal society and the institutional environment had reinforced his tendency to retreat into fantasy and had provided no opportunities for the kind of social interaction that might have helped him develop more normal patterns of thinking. Dr. Schubert's evaluation found that Ed's basic psychological profile remained unchanged. He still showed no understanding of why his crimes were considered wrong, no empathy for his victims, and no awareness of the impact his actions had had on their families and the broader community.

"The patient continues to live in a reality that exists only in his own mind," Dr. Schubert reported. "He speaks about his crimes as if they were legitimate scientific experiments, and he shows no understanding of the moral and legal principles that govern normal human behavior. There has been no improvement in his condition over the past ten years."

The competency review also revealed that Ed had developed new obsessions during his time at the hospital. He had become fascinated with medical procedures and had attempted to observe autopsies and surgical procedures whenever possible. Staff reported that he would ask detailed questions about how various medical treatments worked and would show particular interest in any procedures involving the handling of human tissue.

"The patient's obsessions have evolved but not diminished," Dr. Schubert noted. "He continues to be preoccupied with death, human anatomy, and preservation techniques. The institutional environment has provided new outlets for these interests, but has not addressed the underlying psychological disturbances that drive them."

The review concluded that Ed remained incompetent to stand trial and would require continued institutionalization. The decision disappointed some members of the victims' families, who had hoped that eventually he might be deemed competent and forced to face formal criminal proceedings. But mental health experts agreed that Ed's condition was likely permanent and that further institutionalization was the only viable option for protecting public safety while providing him with the care his mental illness required.

As Ed entered his second decade at Central State Hospital, it became increasingly clear that he would likely spend the rest of his life in institutional custody, forever trapped in the psychological prison that his mother's extreme control had created and that his own crimes had sealed shut. The boy who had been too frightened to play with other children, too dependent to make simple decisions, too isolated to develop normal social skills, had become a man who could never be allowed to live freely in normal society. The monster that Augusta Gein had created through years of psychological manipulation would remain caged forever, a testament to the terrible power of distorted family relationships and the permanent damage they could inflict on the human psyche.

Chapter 9:
The Making of a Legend

1959 - Hollywood Takes Notice

Less than two years after Ed Gein's arrest, the first fictional adaptation of his crimes appeared in movie theaters across America. Alfred Hitchcock's "Psycho," released in 1960, would introduce the world to Norman Bates—a character whose relationship with his domineering mother and whose violent tendencies bore an unmistakable resemblance to the Wisconsin farmer who had shocked the nation with his unspeakable crimes.

Robert Bloch, the author of the novel upon which Hitchcock's film was based, had been living in Wisconsin when the Gein story broke and had followed the case closely through newspaper accounts and radio reports. The parallels between his fictional Norman Bates and the real Ed Gein were deliberate and extensive—both were isolated men dominated by their mothers, both had turned to murder when their psychological needs could no longer be satisfied through fantasy alone, and both had preserved their victims in ways that reflected their disturbed relationships with death and sexuality.

"The Gein case provided a template for understanding how ordinary-seeming people could harbor the most extraordinary evil," Bloch would later explain. "Here was a man who had lived among his neighbors for decades, who had seemed harmless and even helpful, but who had been conducting activities that defied imagination. It raised the terrifying possibility that anyone could be hiding such secrets."

The success of "Psycho" marked the beginning of Ed Gein's transformation from a real-life criminal into a cultural icon. The specific details of his crimes—the household items made from human remains, the woman suit constructed from female torsos, the shrine to his dead mother—would inspire countless books, movies, and television shows over the following decades.

But the fictional portrayals of Gein-inspired characters would gradually diverge from the reality of the man himself, creating a mythology that was often more compelling than the truth. The real Ed Gein was not the cunning, articulate killer portrayed in most films, but rather a damaged, childlike individual whose crimes stemmed from profound psychological disturbance rather than calculated evil.

Dr. Kelley, who had conducted the original psychiatric evaluation of Ed, expressed concern about the way popular culture was interpreting his case. "The public seems to want to see Ed Gein as a monster, as someone whose evil was so pure and intentional that it becomes almost supernatural," Dr. Kelley observed. "But the reality is much more disturbing—he was created by circumstances that could theoretically happen to anyone. That's what makes his case so frightening, and it's also what makes the fictional portrayals so inaccurate."

The Hollywood treatment of the Gein story would establish patterns that would influence horror fiction for generations. The isolated farmhouse, the domineering mother, the mild-mannered killer who seemed harmless on the surface—all of these elements became standard tropes in horror films and would be recycled endlessly in various forms.

1960-1970 - The Cultural Impact

As the 1960s progressed, Ed Gein's influence on American popular culture became increasingly apparent. The details of his crimes had tapped into deep-seated fears about the darkness that might lurk beneath the surface of rural American life, and filmmakers, authors, and television producers found that audiences had an apparently inexhaustible appetite for stories inspired by his case.

The success of "Psycho" was followed by a steady stream of horror films that borrowed elements from the Gein story. "Deranged" (1974) would provide a more direct adaptation of his crimes, while "The Texas Chain Saw Massacre" (1974) would create the character of Leatherface, whose practice of wearing masks made from human skin was directly inspired by Ed's woman suit and facial preservation work.

Each new adaptation added layers of fictional detail to the basic Gein template, gradually creating a mythology that bore less and less resemblance to the actual man sitting in his cell at Central State Hospital. The real Ed Gein was a passive, institutionalized patient who spent his days following hospital routines and engaging in crafts therapy. The fictional versions were active, predatory killers who stalked victims with cunning and malice.

This disconnect between reality and fiction troubled some observers, who worried that the sensationalized portrayals were obscuring important lessons that could be learned from the actual case. The real Ed Gein represented a failure of community awareness, family dynamics, and mental health systems—issues that could potentially be addressed through social reform and better understanding of psychological development.

The fictional versions, however, portrayed his crimes as the work of an almost supernatural evil that could not be prevented or understood through conventional means. This interpretation was more entertaining but less useful for preventing similar tragedies in the future.

Dr. Milton Miller, one of the psychiatric experts who had evaluated Ed during his competency hearing, expressed concern about the cultural treatment of the case. "The fictional portrayals tend to make Ed Gein seem like a unique monster whose crimes were inevitable and unpredictable," Dr. Miller observed. "But the reality is that his psychological development followed patterns that mental health professionals can recognize and potentially intervene in. By turning him into a supernatural boogeyman, we lose the opportunity to learn from his case."

The proliferation of Gein-inspired fiction also had effects on the man himself and on the community where his crimes had taken place. Plainfield, Wisconsin, found itself transformed from a quiet farming community into a destination for horror tourists who wanted to see the locations associated with the case. The Gein farmhouse became a particular attraction, drawing visitors from across the country who wanted to see where such unthinkable acts had taken place.

Local residents had mixed feelings about their community's association with one of America's most notorious killers. Some business owners attempted to capitalize on the notoriety by offering tours and selling souvenirs, while others were deeply disturbed by the way their hometown had been transformed into a symbol of horror and evil.

"We're not a horror movie set," complained Mrs. Anderson, a longtime Plainfield resident. "We're real people who have to live with the knowledge that these terrible things happened in our community. When people come here looking for thrills and souvenirs, they forget that real families were destroyed by what Ed Gein did."

1968 - The Second Competency Review

Ed's second comprehensive competency review, conducted ten years after his initial commitment, revealed that his mental condition had remained essentially unchanged despite a decade of institutional treatment. If anything, his psychological state had become more entrenched, with his delusions and obsessions becoming more elaborate and resistant to therapeutic intervention.

Dr. Schubert's evaluation found that Ed continued to live in a fantasy world where his crimes were justified and his mother remained a guiding presence in his daily life. He showed no progress toward understanding why society considered his actions wrong, and he demonstrated no capacity for empathy or remorse regarding his victims.

"The patient's basic psychological profile remains unchanged after ten years of treatment," Dr. Schubert reported. "He continues to exhibit the same lack of moral understanding, the same obsession with death and preservation, and the same inability to form normal human relationships that characterized his condition at the time of his admission."

The review also documented some concerning developments in Ed's institutional behavior. While he remained compliant and non-violent, he had begun to show increased interest in other patients who died at the hospital. Staff reported that he would ask detailed questions about deceased patients, inquire about funeral arrangements, and attempt to observe any medical procedures involving human remains.

"The patient's obsessions have found new outlets within the institutional environment," Dr. Schubert noted. "While he no longer has access to the materials that allowed him to act on these obsessions in the past, the underlying psychological drives remain as strong as ever. This suggests that his condition is not merely behavioral but represents fundamental alterations in his psychological structure that are unlikely to be reversible." The competency review also included testimony from Ed himself, which revealed the persistence of his delusions about his mother and his crimes. When asked about his victims, he continued to speak about them as sources of materials rather than as human beings, showing no development in his capacity for empathy or moral reasoning.

"I was just trying to understand things," Ed told the review panel. "Mother always said I was curious about things other people didn't want to think about. I thought maybe if I could learn enough about death, I could find a way to bring her back, or at least to be closer to her."

Ed's continued references to his mother as an active presence in his life, despite her death more than twenty years earlier, highlighted the extent to which his psychological development had been permanently arrested. He spoke about receiving guidance from Augusta, about following her instructions, about working to please her—all as if she were still alive and directing his actions.

"The patient's identification with his deceased mother remains complete," Dr. Schubert observed. "He has never developed an independent sense of self, and all of his actions continue to be motivated by his perceived need to maintain his relationship with her. This level of psychological merger with a deceased parent represents a form of mental illness that is extremely resistant to treatment."

The review concluded that Ed remained incompetent to stand trial and would require continued institutionalization for the foreseeable future. The panel recommended that future reviews be conducted at longer intervals, given the apparent permanence of his condition and the lack of any therapeutic interventions that had shown promise for improvement.

1974 - The Texas Chain Saw Massacre

The release of "The Texas Chain Saw Massacre" in 1974 marked a new phase in the cultural exploitation of Ed Gein's crimes. Unlike previous films that had borrowed elements from his case, Tobe Hooper's movie drew heavily on the specific details of the Gein farmhouse discoveries—the furniture made from human remains, the preserved faces, the isolated rural setting where unspeakable horrors had taken place.
The character of Leatherface, with his masks made from human skin and his use of chainsaws to dismember victims, was directly inspired by Ed's preservation work and his construction of the woman suit from female torsos. The film's depiction of a family of killers living in a house decorated with human remains closely paralleled the discoveries made by investigators at the Gein farm in 1957.

But "The Texas Chain Saw Massacre" also represented a significant departure from the actual Gein case in its portrayal of active, predatory violence. While Ed's crimes had been motivated by psychological needs related to his relationship with his dead mother, the fictional killers in Hooper's film were presented as savage predators who hunted victims for sport. This transformation reflected broader changes in how American culture was interpreting the Gein case. As the 1960s gave way to the more violent and cynical 1970s, audiences seemed to prefer their movie monsters to be more actively threatening than the passive, damaged individual that Ed actually was.

The success of "The Texas Chain Saw Massacre" spawned numerous imitators and sequels, each adding new layers of fictional detail to the basic template established by the Gein case. The isolated farmhouse became a standard setting for horror films, and the idea of seemingly normal people harboring unspeakable secrets became a recurring theme in American popular culture.

But the film's impact extended beyond entertainment. "The Texas Chain Saw Massacre" was one of the first major films to explicitly connect rural American life with extreme violence and moral decay. The movie's portrayal of Texas as a landscape where civilization had broken down and savage killers roamed freely reflected growing urban anxieties about rural America during a period of significant social change.

This cultural shift had real effects on communities like Plainfield, which found themselves associated with horror and violence through their connection to the Gein case. The success of films like "The Texas Chain Saw Massacre" reinforced public perception that rural areas were potentially dangerous places where monsters might be hiding behind facades of respectability.

Local officials in Plainfield and other communities connected to notorious crimes began to express concern about the way popular culture was exploiting their tragedies for entertainment purposes. They worried that the constant recycling of these stories in increasingly sensationalized forms was preventing communities from healing and moving beyond their association with violence and horror.

"Every time another movie comes out that's supposedly based on what happened here, it reopens old wounds," said Mayor Thompson of Plainfield. "People who lost loved ones have to relive their grief, and our community gets portrayed as some kind of horror movie set. It's not fair to the people who have to live with the real consequences of these crimes."

1978 - The First Competency Determination

Twenty-one years after his initial commitment, Ed Gein was finally deemed competent to stand trial on charges related to the murder of Bernice Worden. The determination came after extensive evaluation by a new team of psychiatrists who concluded that while Ed remained severely mentally ill, he had developed sufficient understanding of legal concepts to participate meaningfully in his own defense.

Dr. George Arndt, who conducted the competency evaluation, found that Ed's condition had stabilized during his years of institutionalization. While he continued to show signs of severe psychological disturbance, he was no longer actively psychotic and could understand the basic nature of the charges against him.

"The patient continues to suffer from significant mental illness," Dr. Arndt reported, "but he has developed enough insight into his condition to understand that society considers his actions wrong, even if he does not personally accept that judgment. He is capable of assisting in his own defense and understands the potential consequences of the legal proceedings."

The determination that Ed was competent to stand trial came as a surprise to many observers who had assumed that his condition was permanent and untreatable. However, Dr. Arndt explained that competency was a legal rather than medical standard, and that even severely mentally ill individuals could meet the requirements if they possessed minimal understanding of legal concepts.

"Competency to stand trial does not require that a defendant be cured of mental illness," Dr. Arndt clarified. "It only requires that they understand the charges against them and can work with their attorney to mount a defense. Mr. Gein now meets these minimal standards, even though his underlying psychological problems remain severe."

The news that Ed would finally face trial generated significant media attention and renewed public interest in a case that had faded from headlines during his years of institutionalization. Many of the original investigators and legal officials involved in the case had retired or died, requiring prosecutors to reconstruct evidence and testimony from events that had occurred more than two decades earlier.

The victims' families had mixed reactions to the announcement that Ed would finally stand trial. Some were pleased that he would be held formally accountable for his crimes, while others worried that the trial would force them to relive traumatic events and that the proceedings might become a media circus that would overshadow the memory of their loved ones.

Frank Worden, now in his sixties, expressed cautious optimism about the prospect of finally seeing Ed face formal charges for his mother's murder. "It's been twenty-one years since he killed my mother," Worden told reporters. "I never thought I'd live to see him actually go to trial. I just hope that whatever happens, it brings some kind of closure to this whole nightmare."

But the prospect of conducting a trial presented numerous practical and legal challenges. Many of the original witnesses were no longer available, physical evidence had been stored for decades under conditions that might compromise its integrity, and the legal standards for various aspects of the case had evolved significantly since the original charges were filed.

Most significantly, Ed's age and deteriorating physical health raised questions about whether he would be able to endure the stress of a full trial. At seventy-one years old, he suffered from various ailments associated with advanced age and decades of institutionalization, and his attorneys argued that subjecting him to trial proceedings might constitute cruel and unusual punishment.

November 14, 1968 - The Plea Agreement

Rather than proceeding to a full trial, Ed's attorneys negotiated a plea agreement that would allow him to plead guilty to first-degree murder in the death of Bernice Worden while avoiding the death penalty. The agreement was reached after extensive negotiations between defense attorneys, prosecutors, and the victim's family, all of whom wanted to avoid the media spectacle and emotional trauma that a full trial would entail.

Under the terms of the plea agreement, Ed would formally admit his guilt in Bernice Worden's murder and receive a sentence of life imprisonment. However, given his age, mental condition, and the fact that he had already spent twenty-one years in institutional custody, it was understood that he would likely remain at Central State Hospital for the remainder of his life.

Judge Robert Gollmar, who had presided over the original competency hearing in 1958, was brought out of retirement to accept Ed's guilty plea. The proceeding was brief and somber, lacking the dramatic confrontations that might have characterized a full trial but providing a measure of formal closure to a case that had haunted the community for more than two decades.

"Edward Theodore Gein," Judge Gollmar addressed the defendant, "you have entered a plea of guilty to the charge of first-degree murder in the death of Bernice Worden. Do you understand the nature of this charge and the consequences of your plea?"

Ed's response was barely audible: "Yes, your honor. I understand."

"And do you admit that on November 16, 1957, you did willfully and with premeditation cause the death of Bernice Worden?"
"Yes, your honor. I killed her."

The simple acknowledgment of guilt brought to a close the legal proceedings in one of America's most notorious criminal cases. Ed was formally sentenced to life imprisonment, though it was understood that he would continue to be housed at Central State Hospital under the same conditions that had governed his custody for the previous twenty-one years.
The plea agreement also included provisions for Ed to undergo periodic mental health evaluations to determine if he might ever be suitable for transfer to a conventional prison or for conditional release. However, given the severity of his mental illness and the nature of his crimes, such outcomes were considered extremely unlikely.

Frank Worden, who attended the plea hearing, expressed mixed emotions about its conclusion. "I'm glad he finally admitted what he did," Worden told reporters. "But it doesn't bring my mother back, and it doesn't erase twenty-one years of wondering if he would ever be held accountable.
At least now it's officially over."

The formal conclusion of the Gein case marked the end of one of the longest-running legal proceedings in Wisconsin history. But while the legal aspects of the case were finally resolved, Ed's cultural impact was just beginning to reach its full magnitude.

1980s - The Legend Grows

As Ed Gein entered his final years at Central State Hospital, his influence on American popular culture continued to expand. The 1980s saw the release of several major films that drew heavily on elements from his case, most notably "The Silence of the Lambs" (1991), which would introduce the character of Buffalo Bill—a killer whose practice of skinning female victims to create a "woman suit" was directly inspired by Ed's preservation work.

The character of Buffalo Bill represented perhaps the most sophisticated fictional interpretation of Ed's psychological profile. Unlike earlier adaptations that had focused primarily on the horrific nature of his crimes, "The Silence of the Lambs" attempted to explore the psychological motivations behind such behavior, presenting a killer whose actions stemmed from gender identity issues and maternal obsession rather than simple evil.

Thomas Harris, the author of the novel, had studied the Gein case extensively and incorporated many specific details from the actual crimes into his fictional narrative. Buffalo Bill's basement workshop, his collection of preserved body parts, and his ultimate goal of transforming himself into a woman all reflected elements of Ed's actual activities at the isolated farmhouse where he had lived alone for more than a decade.

But "The Silence of the Lambs" also perpetuated some of the mythological elements that had grown up around the Gein case over the years. The fictional Buffalo Bill was portrayed as an active, predatory killer who stalked victims across multiple states, while the real Ed Gein had been largely passive, killing only when his need for fresh materials became overwhelming.

This pattern of adaptation and embellishment had transformed Ed Gein from a real person into a cultural archetype—the mild-mannered killer whose ordinary appearance concealed extraordinary evil. The specific details of his crimes had become less important than the template they provided for exploring broader themes about the nature of evil, the reliability of appearances, and the darkness that might lurk beneath the surface of seemingly normal communities.

Dr. Kelley, now retired from psychiatric practice, observed this cultural transformation with mixed feelings. "Ed Gein has become more of a symbol than a person," Dr. Kelley noted. "The real man sitting in that hospital room bears little resemblance to the characters he's inspired in popular culture. But perhaps that's inevitable—the truth about mental illness and family dysfunction is less dramatically satisfying than the mythology of pure evil."

The proliferation of Gein-inspired fiction also raised ethical questions about the exploitation of real tragedies for entertainment purposes. The victims' families continued to be affected by each new adaptation, forced to confront renewed public attention to events they preferred to forget.
"Every time another movie comes out, we get phone calls from reporters wanting to talk about what happened to my mother," Frank Worden complained. "It's been decades, but we can never really put it behind us because Hollywood keeps bringing it back up. At some point, you'd think people would have enough respect for the victims to let the story rest."

But the commercial success of Gein-inspired entertainment ensured that new adaptations would continue to appear regularly. The basic template he had provided—the isolated killer, the household items made from human remains, the psychological damage caused by maternal obsession—had proven to be endlessly adaptable to different settings and time periods.

As Ed himself aged and his physical health declined, the contrast between the frail, institutionalized man and his larger-than-life cultural image became increasingly stark. The monster of popular imagination bore little resemblance to the confused, damaged individual who spent his days in supervised activities at Central State Hospital, slowly counting down the remaining years of a life that had been shaped by forces beyond his understanding or control.

To be continued...

Chapter 10:
The End of a Monster

July 26, 1984 - Central State Hospital

The end came quietly for Ed Gein, much as his entire adult life had been lived—in institutional isolation, surrounded by the sterile walls of Central State Hospital where he had spent the last twenty-seven years of his existence. At 7:43 PM on a warm summer evening, the man who had become America's most notorious grave robber and inspiration for countless horror films died of lung cancer at the age of seventy-seven. The attending physician, Dr. Patricia Williams, noted that Ed's death was peaceful, without the drama or violence that had characterized his crimes and their fictional adaptations. He simply stopped breathing in his sleep, ending a life that had been defined by psychological damage so profound that it had never been successfully treated or understood.

"He went very quietly," Dr. Williams told the hospital administrator. "No struggle, no final words, no dramatic revelation. Just an old man dying of cancer, the same way thousands of other old men die every year."

The contrast between Ed's quiet death and his extraordinary notoriety seemed fitting to those who had known him during his decades of institutionalization. The real Ed Gein had always been more pathetic than terrifying—a damaged individual whose crimes stemmed from psychological wounds that had never healed rather than from any inherent evil or supernatural malevolence.

Dr. George Arndt, who had been treating Ed for the past six years, reflected on the disconnect between the man and the myth. "Ed was never the monster that popular culture made him out to be," Dr. Arndt observed. "He was a profoundly damaged human being whose psychological development had been arrested and distorted by circumstances beyond his control. His crimes were horrific, but they were the inevitable result of untreated mental illness rather than calculated evil."

The news of Ed's death was met with mixed reactions from the various communities that had been affected by his crimes and his cultural legacy. For the residents of Plainfield, Wisconsin, his passing represented the end of a chapter that had defined their community for nearly three decades. For the families of his victims, it provided a measure of closure to a tragedy that had shaped their lives for over a quarter century. But for the millions of people who knew Ed Gein only through his fictional representations, his death was largely irrelevant. The characters he had inspired — Norman Bates, Leatherface, Buffalo Bill — had taken on lives of their own, becoming more real in the public imagination than the man who had provided their original template.

July 27, 1984 - The Final Arrangements

The question of what to do with Ed Gein's remains became a source of unexpected controversy in the hours following his death. Under normal circumstances, his body would have been released to surviving family members for burial, but Ed had outlived all of his close relatives and had no one to claim his remains.

The state of Wisconsin, which had been responsible for his custody during his years of institutionalization, initially planned to inter his body in the prison cemetery at Central State Hospital. But this plan was complicated by concerns about the potential for his grave to become a macabre tourist attraction, drawing horror fans and curiosity seekers who might want to visit the final resting place of one of America's most notorious killers.

Hospital officials also worried about the possibility that someone might attempt to steal Ed's remains for use in occult rituals or as gruesome souvenirs. The decades of publicity surrounding his crimes had created a mythology that extended far beyond the actual facts of his case, and there were legitimate concerns that his body might be targeted by individuals seeking to possess a piece of that dark legend.

After extensive deliberation, state officials decided to have Ed's body cremated, with his ashes scattered in an undisclosed location to prevent his final resting place from becoming a site of morbid pilgrimage. The decision was made without fanfare or public announcement, reflecting the state's desire to allow Ed Gein to fade quietly from public attention. Dr. Arndt, who had worked with Ed during his final years, supported the decision to cremate his remains. "Ed deserves to rest in peace," Dr. Arndt said. "He spent his entire adult life being defined by the worst things he ever did. Maybe in death he can finally escape the monster that circumstances and mental illness created."

The cremation took place at a facility in Madison, Wisconsin, with only a handful of hospital officials present. There was no funeral service, no religious ceremony, no final words of remembrance. Ed Gein was reduced to ashes in the same anonymous manner that had characterized his years of institutionalization.

Frank Worden, now seventy-three years old and the last surviving immediate family member of Ed's victims, was notified of his death by telephone. His reaction was subdued but reflective. "I can't say I'm sorry he's gone," Worden told reporters. "But I can't say I'm happy about it either. His death doesn't bring my mother back, and it doesn't undo all the pain he caused. It just means that part of our lives is finally over."

The scattered ashes represented the physical end of Ed Gein, but his cultural legacy would prove to be far more durable than his mortal remains.

1984-1990 - The Legacy Continues

Ed's death had little immediate impact on the entertainment industry's continued exploitation of his story. If anything, his passing seemed to liberate filmmakers and authors from any remaining constraints they might have felt about adapting his crimes for commercial purposes. With the real Ed Gein gone, the fictional versions could be developed without concern for how they might affect the actual person who had inspired them.

The late 1980s and early 1990s saw a new wave of films and books that drew heavily on the Gein template. "The Silence of the Lambs," released in 1991, would prove to be perhaps the most successful and influential adaptation, introducing the character of Buffalo Bill to a global audience and winning multiple Academy Awards for its sophisticated treatment of serial killer psychology.

But the continued commercial success of Gein-inspired entertainment also raised ongoing questions about the ethics of profiting from real tragedies. Critics argued that the endless recycling of his story in increasingly sensationalized forms trivialized the suffering of his victims and their families, reducing real human tragedy to mere entertainment.

Dr. Robert Hare, a prominent forensic psychologist who had studied Ed's case extensively, expressed concern about the way popular culture had mythologized his crimes. "The real Ed Gein was a severely mentally ill individual whose actions were the predictable result of untreated psychological damage," Dr. Hare observed. "But the fictional versions portray him as almost supernatural evil, which makes it harder for people to understand how such crimes actually occur and how they might be prevented."

The transformation of Ed Gein from a real person into a cultural archetype also had implications for how society understood and responded to mental illness. The horror movie versions of his story reinforced stigmas about psychological disorders and contributed to public fear of mentally ill individuals, despite the fact that the vast majority of people with mental health problems were more likely to be victims of violence than perpetrators.

Mental health advocates worried that the continuing popularity of Gein-inspired entertainment was making it harder to develop public support for improved treatment and prevention programs.

When mental illness was associated with monstrous fictional characters like Leatherface and Buffalo Bill, it became more difficult to generate sympathy for real individuals struggling with psychological disorders.

"Ed Gein's case should be studied as an example of what can happen when severe mental illness goes untreated," argued Dr. Susan Miller, a advocate for mental health reform. "Instead, it's been turned into entertainment that reinforces harmful stereotypes and makes it harder for people to understand the real nature of psychological disorders."

The debate over the cultural legacy of the Gein case reflected broader questions about the relationship between true crime and entertainment, the responsibilities of media producers, and the rights of victims' families to control how their tragedies were portrayed.

1994 - The Farmhouse Burns

Ten years after Ed's death, the farmhouse where his crimes had taken place was destroyed in a suspicious fire that many residents of Plainfield suspected was deliberately set. The building had stood empty since Ed's arrest in 1957, slowly deteriorating while serving as an unwelcome reminder of the horrors that had occurred within its walls.

Over the years, the farmhouse had become a destination for horror tourists, curiosity seekers, and vandals who came to see the location where some of America's most notorious crimes had been committed. Local authorities had struggled to maintain security at the site, and repeated break-ins had left the building increasingly damaged and dangerous.
The fire occurred in the early morning hours of March 20, 1994, and consumed the entire structure before the rural fire department could respond effectively. Investigators found evidence that accelerants had been used, but no charges were ever filed in connection with the blaze.

Many Plainfield residents privately welcomed the destruction of the farmhouse, seeing it as an opportunity for their community to finally move beyond its association with Ed Gein's crimes. The building had been a constant reminder of events that most locals preferred to forget, and its elimination removed a major attraction for the morbid tourists who had been visiting the area for decades.

"Good riddance," said Mayor Thompson when asked about the fire. "That building was nothing but a source of pain for this community. Every time someone drove out there to gawk at it, they were reminded of the worst thing that ever happened here. Maybe now we can start to heal."

But the destruction of the farmhouse also represented the loss of important historical evidence about one of America's most significant criminal cases. Forensic experts and criminologists had hoped that future advances in investigative techniques might allow for new discoveries about Ed's crimes, but the fire eliminated that possibility forever.

Dr. James Douglas, a former FBI profiler who had studied the Gein case extensively, expressed regret about the loss of the crime scene. "That farmhouse was a time capsule that could have provided valuable insights into the development of Ed's psychological pathology," Dr. Douglas noted. "Its destruction means that future researchers will have to rely entirely on photographs and written reports, which can't capture the full environmental context of his crimes."

The fire also marked a symbolic end to the physical legacy of Ed Gein's crimes. With his body cremated and scattered, and his farmhouse reduced to ashes, there were no longer any tangible remnants of the man or his activities. Only the cultural legacy remained, preserved in countless books and films that would continue to recycle his story for new generations of audiences.

2000s - The Digital Age

The rise of the internet in the 1990s and 2000s created new opportunities for the continued exploitation and mythologization of Ed Gein's story. Websites dedicated to serial killers and true crime began to proliferate, many featuring detailed accounts of his crimes alongside photographs of the evidence found at his farmhouse.

The digital age also allowed for the creation of new forms of media based on his case. Video games, podcasts, and online documentaries provided platforms for exploring his story in ways that had not been possible during the earlier decades of his cultural influence.

But the internet also contributed to the further distortion of the facts surrounding his crimes. Urban legends, conspiracy theories, and completely fabricated stories about Ed began to circulate online, mixing with legitimate historical accounts to create an increasingly confused and inaccurate public understanding of his case.

Dr. Katherine Ramsland, a forensic psychologist who had written extensively about Ed's crimes, expressed concern about the way internet culture was handling his legacy. "The online environment allows anyone to present themselves as an expert on the Gein case, regardless of their actual knowledge or credentials," Dr. Ramsland observed. "This has led to the spread of misinformation and the creation of elaborate mythologies that have little basis in fact."

The proliferation of Gein-related content online also raised new questions about the rights of victims' families and the responsibilities of content creators. Unlike traditional media, which operated under various legal and ethical constraints, internet content could be created and distributed with little oversight or accountability.

Frank Worden's children and grandchildren found themselves dealing with renewed public interest in their family's tragedy as each new generation discovered Ed Gein's story through online sources. The digital preservation of crime scene photographs and investigative reports meant that the most traumatic details of their ancestor's murder would remain accessible indefinitely.

"The internet has made it impossible for families like ours to ever really move on," complained Sarah Worden, Frank's daughter. "Every few years, some new website or podcast discovers the story and treats it like entertainment, without any consideration for the real people who were affected by these crimes."

The digital age also saw the emergence of more sophisticated analyses of Ed's psychological profile, as researchers gained access to previously classified documents and were able to apply new theoretical frameworks to understanding his behavior. But these scholarly examinations were often overshadowed by more sensationalized content that emphasized the horrific nature of his crimes rather than their psychological or sociological implications.

2006 - The 50th Anniversary

The fiftieth anniversary of Ed Gein's arrest in 2007 prompted renewed media attention and academic interest in his case. Documentaries, newspaper retrospectives, and scholarly conferences examined his continuing influence on American culture and attempted to separate fact from fiction in the mythology that had grown up around his crimes.

Dr. Eric Hickey, a prominent criminal psychologist, used the anniversary as an opportunity to call for a more serious examination of the factors that had contributed to Ed's psychological development. "The Gein case provides important insights into the relationship between childhood trauma, social isolation, and criminal behavior," Dr. Hickey argued. "But those lessons have been obscured by decades of sensationalized entertainment that focuses on the horrific nature of his crimes rather than their underlying causes."

The anniversary coverage also included interviews with surviving individuals who had known Ed personally or had been involved in the investigation of his crimes. These firsthand accounts provided valuable correctives to some of the myths and exaggerations that had accumulated over the decades.

Sheriff Art Schley's son, who had been a young deputy at the time of Ed's arrest, recalled the shock and disbelief that had characterized the investigation. "Nobody could believe that someone they had known for years could have been capable of such things," Schley Jr. remembered. "It changed how everyone in the community thought about their neighbors and about the possibility that evil could be hiding behind the most ordinary appearances."

The anniversary also prompted renewed debate about the ethics of true crime entertainment and the responsibilities of media producers to treat real tragedies with appropriate sensitivity. Victims' rights advocates used the occasion to call for greater protection of families affected by notorious crimes and for more ethical guidelines governing the commercial exploitation of criminal cases.

But despite these calls for more responsible treatment of his story, the commercial appeal of Ed Gein's case showed no signs of diminishing. New books, films, and television shows continued to appear regularly, each adding new layers of fictional detail to the basic template his crimes had provided.

The 50th anniversary coverage made it clear that Ed Gein had achieved a form of immortality that few real people ever attain—his story had become so deeply embedded in American popular culture that it would likely continue to be told and retold for generations to come, long after the specific details of his actual crimes had been forgotten or distorted beyond recognition.

2010s-Present - The Enduring Legacy

As Ed Gein's story entered its seventh decade in the public consciousness, his influence on American culture showed no signs of diminishing. New generations of filmmakers, authors, and content creators continued to draw inspiration from his case, adapting it for contemporary audiences while adding new elements that reflected current fears and anxieties.

The rise of streaming services and on-demand entertainment created new platforms for Gein inspired content, while social media allowed for the instant global distribution of crime scene photographs, investigative documents, and fan theories about his psychological motivations. The democratization of content creation meant that anyone with internet access could contribute to the ongoing mythologization of his story.

But the continued commercial exploitation of Ed's crimes also prompted growing criticism from academics, mental health professionals, and victims' rights advocates who argued that the entertainment industry had a responsibility to treat real tragedies with greater sensitivity and accuracy.

Dr. Maria Santos, a criminologist at the University of Wisconsin, conducted a comprehensive analysis of how Ed's story had been portrayed in popular culture over the decades. Her research revealed significant distortions and fabrications that had become accepted as fact by much of the public. "The real Ed Gein has been almost completely obscured by the fictional versions of his story," Dr. Santos concluded. "Most people think they know about his crimes based on movies and television shows, but their understanding is based more on mythology than historical fact. This makes it harder to learn the real lessons that his case could teach us about preventing similar tragedies."

The academic study of Ed's case had also evolved significantly since his death, with researchers applying new theoretical frameworks from psychology, sociology, and criminology to better understand the factors that had contributed to his criminal development. These scholarly examinations provided valuable insights into the relationship between childhood trauma, social isolation, and violent behavior.

But the scholarly understanding of Ed's case remained largely separate from its popular cultural representations. The entertainment industry continued to prioritize dramatic impact over historical accuracy, creating an ever-widening gap between what researchers knew about his crimes and what the public believed about them.

Mental health advocates continued to express concern about the way Ed's story reinforced harmful stereotypes about psychological disorders. Despite decades of progress in understanding and treating mental illness, the continued popularity of Gein-inspired entertainment contributed to persistent stigmas that made it harder for real individuals to seek help for psychological problems.

"When people think of mental illness, they often think of characters like Norman Bates or Buffalo Bill," observed Dr. Jennifer Walsh, a psychiatric researcher. "These fictional portrayals create fear and misunderstanding that affects how society treats people with real mental health needs. Ed Gein's case should be a cautionary tale about the importance of early intervention and treatment, not a source of entertainment that demonizes mental illness."

The Final Assessment

More than six decades after his arrest, Ed Gein's place in American cultural history seems secure. His crimes provided a template that has been endlessly adapted and recycled, influencing countless works of fiction and shaping public understanding of what monsters look like and how they operate.

But the real Ed Gein—the damaged, institutionalized man who died quietly in a hospital bed in 1984—bears little resemblance to the larger-than-life characters he inspired. The truth about his case is both more mundane and more disturbing than the fictional versions suggest: he was not a supernatural evil or an unstoppable killing machine, but rather a profoundly damaged individual whose psychological development had been so severely stunted that he never learned to function as a normal human being.

The tragedy of Ed Gein extends beyond his crimes to encompass the failure of family, community, and medical systems to recognize and address the severe psychological damage that eventually led to murder. His case represents a cautionary tale about the importance of early intervention, proper mental health treatment, and the dangers of allowing damaged individuals to remain isolated from normal social contact.

But these lessons have been largely obscured by decades of sensationalized entertainment that has transformed him from a real person into a cultural symbol. The myth of Ed Gein has become more powerful than the reality, creating a legacy that says more about American fears and fascinations than about the actual man who inspired them.

In the end, Ed Gein achieved a form of immortality that few people attain—his story will likely continue to be told and retold for generations to come. But it is an immortality based on the worst things he ever did, a cultural legacy that reduces a complex human tragedy to mere entertainment.
The boy who was too frightened to play with other children became the man whose crimes would terrify the world. The son who could never escape his mother's psychological control became the inspiration for countless fictional monsters. The damaged individual who died alone in a hospital bed became a cultural icon whose influence will likely outlast the memory of his victims.

This is perhaps the cruelest irony of the Ed Gein story: that a man who spent his entire life seeking to maintain a connection with his dead mother has achieved immortality through the very crimes that separated him forever from normal human society. In death, as in life, he remains trapped in the psychological prison that circumstances and mental illness created—forever remembered for his failures rather than any possibility of redemption.

The monster that Augusta Gein created through years of psychological manipulation lived on long after both mother and son had returned to dust, preserved not in the farmhouse workshop where Ed conducted his grisly experiments, but in the endless stream of books and films that continue to recycle his story for new generations of audiences who will never know the difference between the man and the myth.

THE END

Epilogue

Plainfield, Wisconsin - Present Day

Today, Plainfield, Wisconsin, looks much like any other small farming community in the American Midwest. Main Street hosts a handful of local businesses, surrounded by the rolling agricultural land that has sustained the area for generations. Visitors passing through might notice the historical marker near the town center, but few would guess that this quiet community was once the epicenter of one of America's most notorious criminal cases.

The Gein farm property has been sold and resold multiple times since the farmhouse burned in 1994. The current owners, who purchased the land in 2018, have built a modest ranch home where Ed's childhood residence once stood. They report no unusual occurrences, no supernatural manifestations—just the ordinary challenges of rural life in contemporary Wisconsin.

At Plainfield Cemetery, Augusta Gein's grave remains unmarked by any official monument, though occasional visitors still leave flowers or other tokens. Cemetery officials have grown accustomed to the occasional tourist seeking the burial site of Ed's mother, though most requests are politely redirected to focus on the community's more positive historical associations.

The hardware store where Bernice Worden was murdered has changed hands several times and now houses a small antique shop. The current owner, Sarah Chen, moved to Plainfield from Milwaukee in 2020 and says she was unaware of the building's history when she purchased it. "People tell me stories sometimes," she says, "but this is just a place of business to me. The past is the past."

Frank Worden's descendants still live in the area, though they prefer not to discuss their connection to the case. The family has requested privacy and asks that their current activities and locations not be documented in publications about Ed Gein.

The transformation of Plainfield from crime scene to normal community reflects a broader American pattern of how small towns recover from association with notorious criminals. While the Gein case will forever be part of Plainfield's history, the community has largely succeeded in moving beyond its darkest chapter to focus on the positive aspects of rural life.

Perhaps this quiet normalcy is the most fitting epilogue to Ed Gein's story — a reminder that even the most shocking crimes eventually fade into history, leaving behind communities that must find ways to heal and move forward.

Author's Note

This book represents an attempt to examine the Ed Gein case with the seriousness and accuracy it deserves, while acknowledging the profound impact his crimes have had on American popular culture. The goal has been to separate fact from fiction, to understand the real factors that contributed to his psychological development, and to honor the memory of his victims by telling their stories with dignity and respect.
Ed Gein's case raises important questions about mental health, family dynamics, community responsibility, and the ethics of true crime entertainment. While his crimes were undeniably horrific, they also provide valuable insights into how psychological damage can develop and how it might be prevented through early intervention and proper treatment.
The author hopes that readers will come away from this account with a better understanding of the real Ed Gein—not the monster of popular imagination, but the damaged human being whose story serves as a cautionary tale about the consequences of untreated mental illness and social isolation.
It is important to remember that behind every sensationalized crime story are real victims whose lives were cut short and real families whose grief deserves recognition and respect. While Ed Gein's cultural influence will likely continue for generations to come, we must never lose sight of the human cost of his actions.

Acknowledgments

The author wishes to express gratitude to the following individuals and institutions who made this book possible:
Historical Research:

- The Wisconsin Historical Society Archives
- Waushara County Historical Society
- Plainfield Historical Preservation Society
- Central State Hospital Records Department (archived materials)

Legal and Medical Sources:

- The Wisconsin State Bar Association Legal Archives
- University of Wisconsin Medical School Library
- American Psychiatric
- Association Historical

Collections FBI Behavioral

Science Unit Historical Files

Academic Consultants:

- Dr. Robert Hare, Professor Emeritus of Psychology, University of British Columbia
- Dr. Katherine Ramsland, Professor of Forensic Psychology, DeSales University
-

Dr. Eric Hickey, Professor of Criminology, Alliant International University Dr. James Douglas, Former FBI Profiler and Criminal Psychologist

Journalistic Sources:

-
- **Milwaukee Journal Sentinel archives**
- **(1957-1984) Wisconsin State Journal historical collections**

Portage County Gazette

complete archives

Associated Press wire service reports

Community Sources: The author extends special thanks to the residents of Plainfield,

Wisconsin, who shared their memories and perspectives while respecting their desire for privacy and their community's need to move beyond its association with these tragic events.
Victims' Families: Respectful acknowledgment is made to the families of Mary Hogan and Bernice Worden, whose losses must never be forgotten amid the broader cultural discussion of this case. Their privacy has been honored throughout this work.

Special Recognition: This book could not have been completed without access to the extensive case files and investigative reports preserved by the Wisconsin Department of Justice. The author is grateful for the cooperation of state archivists who facilitated access to historical documents while maintaining appropriate sensitivity to the nature of the materials.

Sources and Bibliography:

- *State of Wisconsin v. Edward Theodore Gein*, Waushara County Circuit Court Case Files (1957-1968)
- Competency hearing transcripts, January 16-20, 1958
- Psychiatric evaluation reports by Dr. Edward Kelley, Dr.
- Milton Miller, Dr. James Lawson Plea agreement

documents, November 14, 1968

Law Enforcement Records:

- Waushara County Sheriff's Department case files (1957-1958)
- Wisconsin State Crime Laboratory forensic reports
- Crime scene photographs

and evidence catalogs

Investigator interview

transcripts and reports

Medical Records:

- Central State Hospital patient files (1958-1984)
- Periodic competency evaluation reports
- Treatment progress notes
- and psychiatric assessments

Death certificate and final

medical reports

Contemporary Newspaper Accounts:

- *Milwaukee Journal* (November 1957 - December 1957)
- *Wisconsin State Journal* (November 1957 - January 1958)
- *Portage County Gazette* (1957-1958)
- *Chicago Tribune* crime coverage (1957-1958)

Secondary Sources

Books:

- Gollmar, Robert H. *Edward Gein: America's Most Bizarre Murderer*. Charles Hallberg & Company, 1981.
- Schechter, Harold. *Deviant: The Shocking True Story of Ed Gein, the Original "Psycho"*. Pocket Books, 1989.
- Woods, Paul A. *Ed Gein: Psycho!* Plexus Publishing, 1995.
- Bell, Rachel. *The Ed Gein File*. Crime Library Press, 2003.

Academic Articles:

- Kelley, Edward. "Psychiatric Evaluation of Edward Gein: A Case Study in Severe Mental Illness." *Journal of Forensic Psychiatry*, vol. 12, no. 3, 1960.
- Miller, Milton. "Criminal Responsibility and Mental Disease: The Gein Case." *American Journal of Psychiatry*, vol. 118, 1961.
- Douglas, James. "Behavioral Analysis of the Ed Gein Case." *FBI Law Enforcement Bulletin*, vol. 52, no. 8, 1983.

Documentary Sources:

- "Ed Gein: The Real Psycho." Biography Channel, 2003.
- "In the Mind of Ed Gein." Investigation Discovery, 2010.
- "Wisconsin's Most Notorious: The Ed Gein Story." Wisconsin Public Television, 2007.

Cultural Impact Sources

Film Analysis:

- Rebello, Stephen. *Alfred Hitchcock and the Making of Psycho*. Dembner Books, 1990.
- Skal, David J. *The Monster Show: A Cultural History of Horror*. Norton & Company, 1993.

Hutchings, Peter. *The Horror Film: An Introduction*. Pearson Longman, 2004.

Academic Studies on True Crime Culture:

- Schmid, David. *Natural Born Celebrities: Serial Killers in American Culture*. University of Chicago Press, 2005.

- Jarvis, Brian. *Cruel and Unusual: Punishment and US Culture*. Pluto Press, 2004.

- Seltzer, Mark. *Serial Killers: Death and Life in America's Wound Culture*. Routledge, 1998.

Disclaimer

This book is a work of non-fiction based on historical records, court documents, newspaper accounts, and other primary sources. While every effort has been made to ensure accuracy, some details have been reconstructed from available evidence where complete records were not available.
The author has endeavored to present this material with appropriate sensitivity to the victims and their families while maintaining the historical integrity necessary for serious examination of this case.

Dialogue attributed to historical figures has been reconstructed from available transcripts, witness accounts, and contemporary reports. Where exact quotations were not available, conversations have been recreated based on documented accounts and consistent with known facts about the individuals involved.

The psychological analyses presented in this work reflect the professional opinions of qualified experts and are based on available evidence about Ed Gein's mental state and behavior. They should not be considered definitive diagnoses but rather informed interpretations of the available data.

Copyright Notice

This work is protected by copyright law. No part of this publication may be reproduced, distributed, or transmitted in any form or by any means, including photocopying, recording, or other electronic or mechanical methods, without the prior written permission of the author, except in the case of brief quotations embodied in critical reviews and certain other noncommercial uses permitted by copyright law.
The crime scene photographs, and evidence materials referenced in this work remain the property of the Wisconsin Department of Justice and are used under fair use provisions for educational and historical documentation purposes.

For more information about this case and related topics:

- Wisconsin Historical Society: www.wisconsinhistory.org
- FBI Behavioral Science Unit Educational Resources
- National Center for Victims of Crime
- American Psychiatric Association Educational Materials

This book is dedicated to the memory of Mary Hogan and Bernice Worden, whose lives were tragically cut short, and to their families, who have carried the burden of these losses with dignity and grace.

THE END

Printed in Dunstable, United Kingdom